COUPLEHOOD

Paul Reiser

COUPLEHOOD

BANTAM BOOKS
SYDNEY • AUCKLAND • TORONTO • NEW YORK • LONDON

COUPLEHOOD

A BANTAM BOOK

First published in Australia and New Zealand in 1995 by Bantam
Reprinted 1995 (twice), 1996 (twice)

National Library of Australia
Cataloguing-in-Publication Entry

Reiser, Paul.
Couplehood

ISBN 1 86359 724 7 (pbk.)

1. American wit and humour.
2. Man-woman relationships – Humour. I. Title.
818.5407

Bantam books are published by

Transworld Publishers (Aust) Pty Limited
15 –25 Helles Ave, Moorebank, NSW 2170

Transworld Publishers (NZ) Limited
3 William Pickering Drive, Albany, Auckland

Transworld Publishers (UK) Limited
61 - 63 Uxbridge Road, Ealing, London W5.55A

Bantam Doubleday Dell Publishing Group Inc
1540 Broadway, New York, New York 10036

Production by Vantage Graphics
Printed in Australia by McPherson's Printing Group

10 9 8 7 6 5

To Paula, who makes the dance so fun.

And so worthwhile.

"Happiness is the quiet lull between problems."

—*My Father*

"Loneliness is when you sneeze
and there's no one there to say 'gesundheit.'"

—*My Mother*

Contents

About the Author

PAUL REISER is the star and co-creator of the critically acclaimed NBC series *Mad About You*. This is his first book. (That he has written. He has read many others—we just don't want to make a big deal out of it.)

Acknowledgments

I want to thank my wife, Paula, without whom I have no act; Dan Strone for asking me if I wanted to write a book; Arthur Spivak for telling me that I did, and making it all happen; my friends and family who put up with me being "so busy because I'm writing a book"; Irwyn Applebaum and all the nice people up at Bantam who made me feel at home; Louie Maggiotto for transcribing and translating; and Rob Weisbach, editor extraordinaire, who took all these shovels full of stuff and made it look very much like a book.

Author's Warning

You will notice in just a second that this book actually begins on page 145. Don't be alarmed—this is not a mistake. Don't try to get your money back. You didn't miss anything.

It's just that I know when *I'm* reading, I love being smack in the middle of the book. Pages behind me, pages ahead of me. It's too overwhelming to know there's so much left and you're only on page 8.

This way, you can read the book for two minutes, and if anybody asks you how far along you are you can say, "I'm on 151—and it's really flying. It just *sails,* baby."

You'll feel like you're accomplishing something, and *I* get credit for writing a bigger book. Everybody wins, and it costs us nothing.

—P.R.
Los Angeles

The

Final

Frontier

———————When I was 12, I remember holding hands with this girl—I want to say, "Patty," but I'm guessing here—and something about the way she held hands was just . . . *wrong*. Our fingers didn't line up right.

You know how when you grab someone's hand, the fingers sort of automatically slide into place, your thumb next to *their* thumb, second finger next to *their* second finger? Simple, right? Not a lot of ways to screw that up. This girl did.

I think what she did was slide her fingers in too *early* so they were all out of sync with mine. (I'm sitting here, holding hands with myself to try to explain this to you.)

145

Okay . . . here's what it is: I like my pinkie to be on the outside. And she started one finger too soon, so *her* pinkie was on the outside, and *my* pinkie was smushed up between her third and fourth fingers.

Now, I'm not saying she's a bad person. But the second we held hands, I knew she wasn't for me. We just didn't *fit*.

And I knew I couldn't explain it to her, either.

Because, the way I figure, there are two types of people: those who *get it* and those who *don't*. If they *get it,* there's nothing to explain, and if they *don't,* there's no point in trying to explain. They don't get it. Move on.

But I remember thinking that if you're going to be with someone, you should find someone who gets it. And someone who fits.

Now, the search for this person starts early. From the minute we're born, boys and girls stare at each other, trying to figure out if they like what they see. Like parade lines, passing each other for mutual inspection. You march, you look. You march, you look. If you're interested, you stop and talk, and if it doesn't work out, you just get back in the parade. You keep marching, and you keep looking.

I was lucky. When I met the woman of my dreams, I

knew. I saw her, and I was immediately unable to speak. My throat locked up, my stomach was in knots, I was sweaty, clammy, and nauseous. I had learned years before that feeling nauseous often means you're in love. (Other times, it simply means you had bad clams, and you want to learn to distinguish between the two.)

But I knew this was it. And the more time we spent together, the more convinced I became—we fit.

Interesting thing: Ask most guys why they marry the woman they do, and they'll tell you, "She's the first one who called me on everything."

All the things you tried to get away with in the past, all the games you designed and mastered for the express purpose of keeping people at arm's length were, it turns out, all just a weeding-out process, a search for the one person who *doesn't* fall for it—the one who can sidestep your tricks and see right through you. And, ironically, you're not upset. In fact, you're impressed. You think, "Wow, good for you." And the message goes forth: "Okay, no more calls, we have a winner."

I remember officially proposing. Actually asking this woman to literally, legally, officially, marry me. I couldn't get the words out. I couldn't stop laughing. It felt so dopey. So cliché. "Asking for her hand in marriage." I felt like I was in some bad Ronald Colman movie.

And it was a moment, after all, I had started planning when I was four and saw a girl jump off the monkey bars and watched her hair bounce off her shoulders. I had given this moment a lot of thought. And suddenly, there it was.

I worried I might do it wrong. Should I be on my knee? Two knees? Should knees even be involved? Should we be somewhere else? Should I have hired a band? Would someone else be doing this better?

But I asked. And for all the silliness, I was amazed when she actually said "Yes." I mean, not that I thought she'd say "No." We'd discussed it. We knew we would be doing this eventually, so popping the question wasn't a real risk. But still, there's something so powerful about a woman saying "Yes." The mutual agreement, the shared desire, the consent—it's staggering.

Think about it. The first time you're intimate with someone, is there anything more exciting than hearing them say "Yes"? It's wild. You can actually get dizzy.

"I could lean and kiss you, and that would be al-right?"

"Yes."

"Really. Hmm . . . You have no problem with this?"

"No."

"You're saying, I could put my hand for example
. . . *here* . . . and that would be alright?"

"Yes."

"Unbelievable."

So there we were, on the brink of the Next Big Thing.
Forever. The Final Frontier. We stared at each other for a
moment, and then I thought, "Uh-oh, if this person's going to be with me *forever,* she's going to find out what I'm
really like. That can't be good."

I mean, she'd already learned *some* things. That's
what the first few years are for; you tiptoe into the water
and reveal the not-so-appealing stuff one thing at a
time.

"You know, don't you, that I won't *always* be wearing cologne? That was really more of a 'while we were
dating' kind of thing."

Start small.

"You know, when I butter a piece of bread, I don't
butter the whole thing. I do each bite separately. Each
piece gets buttered individually."

"I know. I think it's cute."

And then you can tell her the whole story.

"Well, the only reason I bring it up is because I once
lived with a woman who left me because of that. . . . Or
at least that's what she said. I remember, I was in the

middle of buttering a very tiny piece of bread, and she looked at me, swiped the bread out of my hand, and said, 'I don't think this can continue.' . . . It may have been other things, too."

See, a lot of times we're just clueless. We walk around, scarred from previous relationships, thinking we've learned something, when in fact, things that may have been deal breakers in the past may not even *bother* the person you're with now. (Learning what actually bothers the *new* person is how you spend the rest of your life.) But there is this need to disclose potential problem areas.

"I snore."

"That's okay."

"No, but I snore in odd, little rhythms."

"Doesn't bother me."

"I once snored a medley from *The King and I.*"

"My favorite musical."

"Alright. . . . I just thought you should know."

And you keep raising the ante. Not that you want to scare them off; it's just that if they're ever going to leave you, let's get it out of the way now.

"You may notice that in the bathroom, I tend to flush a few seconds before I'm actually done. I don't know why,

I just do. And there's no way I can change. Do you understand this? Can you accept this? Because it has cost me
dearly in the past."

And she *still* hasn't changed her mind.

So you think, "Maybe this'll work." And ultimately, they
find out everything:

How you chew, how you sip, how you hum, how you
dance. How you smell at every point in the day, how you
are on the phone with your mother, the fact that many of
your friends are shallow, that you always have to sit on the
aisle, how you never really listen, how whiny you get when
you travel, how you're not gracious to her friends when
they call, how certain game shows make you really really
happy, how cranky you get because you're too stupid to
remember to eat, how you manage to get confrontational
only when it's with the absolute wrong person to be yelling
at, how you don't like the way you look in any picture
you've taken since 1974, how you're unable to get off the
phone when you're running late because you don't have
the ability to say, "This isn't a good time; can I call you
back?" How you have to lick certain fruits before actually
eating them, how you have no ability to save receipts—all
these things, and they *still* want to sign on. They still like
you.

This feels good. For about a minute.

But the next thought is, "Wait a second, why is she being so understanding? If this stuff doesn't faze her, *her* stuff must be even *worse*. . . . Oh God—what don't *I* know?"

And every day, bit by bit, you find out.

Waking Up Is Hard to Do

Here's how I wake up.

The alarm goes off, I slap it as fast as I can. Whatever song was playing is already stuck in my brain, and I sing it for a while until I realize I don't really know any of the words.

I turn to see my young bride sleeping sweetly, and a series of thoughts comes into my head:

"Isn't she beautiful?"

"Isn't it wonderful I get to see this face I love every morning?"

"Aren't we lucky?"

"Isn't life good?"

"I wonder if my dentist can move my ten o'clock

cleaning to the afternoon, because I want to bring the car in and get the tires checked before lunch."

For the life of me, I don't know how I make this last jump. But I do. Every day. I wake up, it's good, it's good, everything is good, and then—"Boy, I just thought of four things that might go wrong today."

There are just too many things to do.

We all have Things To Do. Big things, little things—doesn't matter. They're things, and they're yours to do.

I'm not particularly organized, but I try to make lists. You can have your Master List of what you're going to do. Or else you have lots of Little Lists, and one Big List, listing all the Little Lists.

"Things to do today." It's always stupid things like "Call cable guy," or "Pick up dry cleaning." This is why you get out of bed that day—to "pick up blue jacket."

Some people have stationery that already says, "Things To Do Today." Why do we need that? The reason you're writing it down in the first place is because you want to do it. I think that's fairly obvious. Who writes down things they *don't* want to do? There are plenty of things I don't want to do. "Don't slam your knee against the dresser drawer." I don't need to write it down. I remember from last time. "Don't eat a piece of melon that's so soft you wouldn't enjoy it." I *know* that.

There are, of course, grander things you want to do with your day, larger goals you have for your life that also don't need to be written down. "Work toward world peace." I don't have to jot that down. "Leave the world better than you found it." I got it, I got it.

So I'm lying there, awake no more than two minutes, already running down my list of Things To Do. My bride is up now, too.

She says, "What are you thinking about?"

"You don't want to know."

I'm still not sure what the rule on that one is. The "tell-me-exactly-what-you're-thinking" thing. Sometimes it's helpful, but generally speaking, not-so-much.

She persists. "Tell me."

"I'm serious, it's too dumb to tell you."

"What?"

"I was just thinking, if they don't have tomato soup at lunch today, I'm not going to get soup at all. Because their other soups are pasty."

A moment of quiet.

"That's what you were thinking about?"

"I told you it wasn't good."

She says, "That's alright, ask me what *I* was thinking about."

"What?"

"The card my sister sent me."

"Would you forget about that card already?"

"Why would she sign it 'Fondly'? She's never used the word 'fondly.' Ever."

"It's the same as 'Love,' only a little . . . fonder."

"I just really don't like that."

So, we've been awake less than eighty seconds, and we're already lost. Whatever sense of magic and wonder there is to the start of a new, fresh day has long ago been shot to hell.

Even if you woke up and *didn't* do this, even if you woke up and heard nothing but the song of the birds and the love in your heart, there's still one moment every morning that's unavoidable and invariably gets your day going wrong.

You know how you get out of bed, drag your feet into the bathroom, flip on the light, and stand in front of the mirror? You know how you squint your eyes and look? *That.* That's the big mistake. Looking in a mirror that early in the day.

It's always a disappointment, no matter who you are. You just see your reflection and think, "That's not what I was hoping for. I could have sworn I was better looking than that. I must be thinking of someone else."

Nobody looks in the mirror and goes, "That's

about right." They always start fixing, moving their hair, tucking their cheeks . . . "No, that's not working either." So you go into the shower, you soap up, clean up, fluff up, dress up, take another look: "Nope, still not working."

It's The Face. Something scientific happens to your face when you sleep. You go to bed normal, you wake up —you have no face. The features have gone away while you slept. I think it has to do with the earth's rotation. As the earth revolves, facial features move with it, so that while you sleep, your face is in Europe. Because there are only a finite number of faces, and if the Europeans go to work with no face, it looks bad for them. So this way everybody gets a shot.

I think it's all nature's way of keeping us humble. At night, you're thinking of your problems, you're thinking of yourself. "How come this didn't work out? How come I live the life I do?"

You wake up, you look in the mirror, and you go, "*That's* why! I have no facial features and a T-shirt with orange juice stains from 1983." It gives you perspective.

First order of business for every couple is negotiating Shower Rights.

"You want to go first?"

"No, *you* go. I'm sleeping."

"Okay, but don't get upset if I use all the hot water."

"Don't."

"I can't control how much hot water comes out—it just comes."

"So get out sooner."

"Alright, I'll try."

"And don't puddle up the floor."

Hmm. "Maybe *you'd* better go first."

My problem is, I like long showers. I enjoy everything that goes on in there. And I get distracted.

I've discovered that while showering, the areas of our body that we spend the most time scrubbing are not necessarily the areas that *need* the most scrubbing. There's a gap between Scrubbing Supply and Scrubbing Demand.

For example, the mid-chest gets an awful lot of scrubbing. Right around the chest plate. We love scrubbing that chestal area. Now the fact is, nobody really ever has dirt there. You couldn't get this part dirty if you wanted to. You'd have to come out of a pool and trip with your arms out. Or eat soup naked and fast.

But we scrub there because it's *convenient.* It's nearby, it doesn't take any effort, you can think about all the Things You Have To Do while you're scrubbing. So we spend forty minutes scrubbing needlessly.

Your *feet,* however, which really need the attention, get nothing. Admit it. Your feet haven't been scrubbed since you were in a bassinet. They're just too far away. No matter how short you are, it's not worth the effort. So you forget about them. "Well, they'll get dripped on. They'll be fine."

Other areas you scrub a lot, not because they're so convenient, but because frankly, it's pleasurable. Certain private areas—they get tremendous attention. The irony is that these are areas thought of as unhygienic, while in fact, they're so clean you could entertain there.

A lot of couples shower together. It's supposed to be romantic and sensual. Truth? It's not all it's cracked up to be. Because one of you is not getting water. One of you, therefore, is not taking a shower.

Let's be honest; one of you is having a great time, it's terrific. The other one is in the back going, "You got a sweater up there? Maybe a windbreaker? Something with a hood would be nice. I would get it, but my ass is frozen to the wall here."

Then there are people who use the shower to do everything. They shave, they brush their teeth, they do their taxes, everything.

I can't shave in a shower. It's too risky. Ever see the guys who shave with an electric razor while they're *driving*? What is *that* about? You telling me there's no other opportunity in their day to have a razor at their throat than while doing sixty around a curve? Surely they could squeeze a moment in before breakfast. Or at least wait for a red light.

Personally, I have to be on dry, non-moving land to shave. And even then, it's not so easy. The main problem is I have no mirror depth perception. It's all distorted; left is right, forward is back—I don't know where I am. Ever try to check the back of your head with another mirror? I can't find myself. I've missed by a good six feet. I go, "Oh, that's not me at all. That's a shower cap on a hook."

The best thing is to find somebody who looks roughly like you and just look at the back of *his* head.

I've actually tried *not* shaving, but it turns out I'm not a Beard Guy. Certain guys look good in beards. I look, at best, like I'm on my way to something that may, ultimately, with a lot of work, *become* a beard.

My beard starts to look promising, and then in four days just gets tired and stops. People see me unshaven and ask, "Oh, what is that—three days, four days?"

And I have to tell them, "Sadly, since last summer. But thank you for caring."

And they always ask. They see stubble and have to comment.

"What are you—growing a beard?"

What if I wasn't? What if I simply forgot to shave? Now they're just criticizing my hygiene. Like if you forgot to shower they'd say, "Hey, did you *mean* to smell like that? You going for some effect or are you just woefully negligent?"

And that awkward stage of Beard Development is toughest on your partner.

"I can't kiss you with that face. It hurts."

"It's going to be a regular beard any day now."

"Let's talk then."

My wife and I start each morning with the genuine intention of exercising. But in a dazzling display of mutual support, we've learned to talk ourselves right out of it.

"Look, *I* don't feel like working out, *you* don't feel like working out—let's just skip it."

"Nobody's going to know, right?"

"It'll be our little secret."

"Right, we'll just look the way we do."

"And if anybody asks, we ran."

The truth is *nobody* wants to work out. We just do it to keep up with people who look better than we do. If we all just agreed to *not* work out—and I mean *everyone,* across the board—we'd be a lot happier. We could eat cupcakes and sleep late. The problem is it would only take *one* guy in good shape to ruin it for the whole group. "Great, now we gotta look like *this* guy. . . ." And the next morning we'd all be back running, lifting, and sweating against our will.

Some people talk like it's nothing. "I'll just lose it after the holidays. It won't be hard—I mean I've only been eating like a pig these last . . . what is it . . . 3 . . . 4 . . . 20 years. I'll have some cottage cheese for lunch, I'll be fine."

We put a lot of pressure on cottage cheese. We've convinced ourselves it's a Miracle Food. If it's on your plate, you're on a diet. Doesn't matter what else is on the plate. It could be three cheeseburgers and a mountain of lard. Drop a scoop of cottage cheese on there—it's a Diet Plate.

Same with a peach half. Somehow it's a Diet Enforcer. "Sixteen pork patties with a piano-size pile of potatoes, and a fresh peach half." And you think, "Peach half —how bad could it be? It's obviously a special Dieter's Platter."

If you ever see cottage cheese *and* half a peach on a plate, for God's sake be careful. You could literally disappear. Your body mass could evaporate into thin air—so powerful are these nutritious diet items.

A footnote: If your partner ever suggests that they have, perhaps, gained an unwanted ounce or two, stay out of it.

I beg you. Even if they bring it up first.

"Do I look a little heavy?"

"No."

"Seriously."

"You don't."

"C'mon, look at this picture from last summer—you gonna tell me I don't look thinner there?"

"Let me see . . . well . . . maybe a little, yeah."

"Oh, like *you're* so perfect?"

"I didn't say anything—you asked!"

"Just drop it."

Hours later: "I can't *believe* you said that."

Now, certain body measurements *never* change. Height and shoe size, for example. These are areas, that, when we were kids, kept growing along with everything else, and then just stopped. No warning. No fanfare; they just hit a number and stayed there.

And back then, getting bigger was a *good* thing. You were proud to be expanding. You showed off your progress. "Look—I'm over four feet already."

Then one day you notice you've been wearing the same sizes several years in a row, and you realize, "I guess I'm done. This is who I am. Five foot ten, and not an inch more. I'm 5'10", 9½ shoe. Forever. That's who I am."

I think it would have been nice to know about it when it happened. You could have had a party.

"Hey, what's everybody celebrating?"

"I finished growing."

"Well, congratulations!! How'd you make out?"

"Five seven and a half, size eight in a dress shoe."

"Good for you."

Let's

Do

Something

————— The need to *do something* can kill you.

You walk into work Monday morning, they're all over you.

"How was your weekend?"

"Have a good weekend?"

"What'd you do with the weekend?"

"Do anything good?"

What the hell could I do that's interesting enough to withstand that kind of pounding? It's a weekend, two days off. How good is it supposed to be?

But they bombard you with How-was-your-weekends, and I feel this great pressure to have *had* a great weekend. For *them*.

"I went skiing, let's say. Would that be enough for you?"

This is what they're looking for. Some kind of action verb.

"We went harpooning. British Columbia."

"We ran a test launch for the space shuttle, alright? Stop grilling me, I tell you!"

Because, invariably, what you do is—nothing. You hang around the house. Read the paper. Take a succession of naps. And even then, people try to make it sound like more.

"So, you relaxed? Took a little R & R?"

"I didn't say I relaxed. I didn't 'R' *or* 'R'. I just did nothing."

And for me, that *is* a great weekend. Doing Nothing. Shutting off the phones, lying on the couch with the woman of my dreams, and just reading—I can't really ask for more than that.

I love reading the paper, and I don't know why. I don't even really read it. I just like to get it, hold it, and look in the general direction of the printed surface. It's the sheer challenge of actually managing to find the time to sit down with a paper that's appealing. That's all it is.

Because the content itself—I'm not all that interested.

Truly. As soon as I sit down with the Sunday Paper, the first thing I do is throw half of it away. Lose the stock reports, lose the grocery coupons, lose the stuff for sale, and lose the travel section. (Where am I going?)

Now you're left with a manageable pile: Sports, magazine section, TV, and regular news.

Here's my thing with the news: I don't know what I'm supposed to do. I don't mean to sound insensitive, it's just that by the time I read about something, it's obviously too late to help. It already happened.

Now, if you told me that *tomorrow* a bus was going to go sailing off the Himalayas, I would get involved. I'd pick up the phone and warn them. "Don't get on the bus. Didn't you see the paper?"

But if I read on Sunday that something happened on Saturday, what can I do? At best I can call to console. "I only just now heard."

Once in a while, I'll actually read the entire paper, so I'll feel like I'm at one with the global community. I know what's going on, I'm okay. I go to sleep. Next morning, the clock radio goes off, and the first thing I hear is, "Good morning. In Jerusalem last night, a bomb went off . . ." and I think, "I can't close my eyes for a minute!"

And I don't understand politics. Like when warring nations call a cease-fire for the holidays. How do they do that? They agree about nothing, but they can still pull it together to go, "Look, we may have our differences, but *nobody* wants to work Christmas."

Why can't they find another reason to hold off one more day?

"Look, the 25th is Christmas and the 26th, I gotta return gifts, I'll be at the stores, the lines—it'll take forever, so the 26th is no good for us."

And then, just keep it going. "The 27th . . . umm, let's see . . . you know, I'd love to resume the hostilities and slaughter your village, but I just noticed—I have the phone guy coming the 27th."

And if you keep your schedule busy enough, things get done *and* you're saving lives right and left.

As a couple, there's something special about reading the paper together. First of all, for some reason, whatever section the other person is reading looks more interesting than the one *you're* reading. Even if you've already read it, you want to see it again.

"I didn't realize how good that Travel section looked till I saw *you* thumbing through it like that. What is that picture there—Portugal?"

I love the fact that we go through the Real Estate

section every Sunday and look at pictures of places we have no intention or possibility of buying, but still we check for price fluctuations.

"Oh, look at this—that lakefront estate in Danbury just went down to *five* bazillion, as opposed to the unreasonable six-two they were asking last month. They're obviously weakening."

Some things in the paper are better *not* to share. But you don't know which ones they are until it's too late.

I'm reading an article about this woman in Houston who was fired, seemingly unfairly, from a very good job. I'm reading, and quietly, to myself, I go, "Hmm . . . tsk . . . geez."

The Woman I Love says, "What's that?"

"Hm? Oh nothing, just this article. This woman, in Houston, she had a great job, and they let her go because they discovered that years earlier she had been a prostitute. . . . Just kind of sad."

She says, "Hmm . . . tsk . . . geez."

A minute and a half later she puts down the Travel section and says, like it's my fault, "What *is* it with prostitutes?"

"What do you mean?"

"I mean, the whole thing with prostitutes and men— I just don't get it."

See, when you're a couple, each person represents their gender. You're the flag bearer for the whole team. And if any member of your team, anywhere in the world, past or present, does something to offend, *you* have to answer for it.

"No, it has nothing to do with prostitutes, Honey, I'm just saying, it's kind of sad . . . You know, here's a woman, got her life together and everything . . . and then . . . hey, what's that picture there, Portugal?" Then you read the Travel section together and try to get off the Houston thing.

But there are aftershocks.

Hours later, we're eating, my loved one turns on me.

"Are you chewing loudly?"

"No."

"Well, you're bugging me."

And I'll think, Let me see, we're chewing, we're eating, chicken, barbecue sauce, Texas— "The prostitute lady? That's what you're upset about?"

She says, "I just don't *get* it."

Even if you're both lounging around, enjoying doing *nothing,* in a heartbeat, it can all go bad.

"I'm bored. Let's do something."

"Like what?"

"I don't care. Anything. I just can't believe we're sitting in our pajamas. Oh, no—we've become one of those couples that never *does* anything. When did this happen? When did we become this dull?"

And my answer is, "I'll tell you when—somewhere in the middle of that article you're reading. Because for a while there, we were doing fine; half-way through the magazine section, we were still happy. But because your article goes bad, it means we're failing as a couple? We are individually and jointly *dull*?"

She says, simply, "We really have to do something."

I Just
Need
Two
Minutes

Getting out of the house is generally harder than doing what you plan to do once you actually *get* out of the house. There are a thousand false starts.

There's the "Who has the keys?"–"*You* had them"–"No, I gave them to *you*" drama, which is always fun.

There's the "Did you leave the machine on?"–"It's not working"–"What do you mean it's not working, let me see" one-act play.

And the ever-popular "Is it going to be cold later?"–"What am I, the weatherman? Just take a jacket and let's go" cartoon.

That's one I particularly enjoy—the jacket dilemma.

My bride, though a remarkably intelligent woman, refuses to accept that the weather at the end of the day is often going to be different than it is now. She becomes a child. "I'm not taking a jacket. I'll be fine." Which relegates *me* to the "just-take-it-and-throw-it-in-the-car-what-the-hell-is-the-big-deal" role.

But there are two opposing forces working here. *She* doesn't want to take the jacket for *vanity* reasons. It's a wardrobe issue. The sweater doesn't go with anything and it makes her look bulky so she'd rather freeze than look bulky and clash.

I, on the other hand, have my own interest in mind. Because I know that later, when she's cold, I'm gonna have to do the Gentleman Thing of taking off my jacket and draping it over her shoulders, for which she'll love me and I will resent her deeply.

Understand: If we were caught in a surprise hailstorm, or the country was invaded and we had to flee suddenly with only what we had on, I would have no problem. I would give her my jacket instinctively. Sure, I'd freeze, but I'd be a hero. I'd be getting something out of it.

But here, we have a choice. It's not hailing. We're not fleeing. We're standing in front of a closet with a myriad of jackets and sweaters and coats and protective gear for every potential five-degree variance—but no, "I'll be fine," she says.

So we go. And of course, later, it's freezing, and

she's huddling in my jacket, and *I,* who knew to bring a jacket, am wearing *no* jacket. And the kicker is: It's not like my jacket looks so good on her anyway. It certainly looks worse than whatever jacket of her *own* she would have put on. But somehow it's okay, because people know what's going on. They won't judge her. When you see a woman with a wildly mismatched jacket draped over her shoulders, you never say, "Boy, what was *she* thinking? That doesn't go at *all.*" You say, "Wow, isn't *he* sweet. Look how he sacrificed his own jacket for her."

And what *I'm* thinking is, "I'm a schmuck. I'm a schmuck, and I'm freezing. I actually thought this through, I planned ahead, and I'm *still* freezing."

Getting dressed is a fascinating little world once you're married. Especially for men. Because upon marriage, you lose the ability to choose clothing by yourself.

I don't know when it happened, but it did. I don't have it anymore. I used to get dressed by myself all the time. I would put on a shirt and pants and go out. In public. And it was not a problem. Nobody was laughing; there was no chuckling behind my back. The fashion police were not knocking down my door. I was fine.

Then, you live with a woman, you get as far as the

door, and you hear, "You're not going to wear that, are you? Tell me you're not going to wear that, because I will leave you right now. The fact that you would even *think* to put those things together frightens me to no end."

And you have to think fast.

"Oh, *together*? No, no, no, no, no. I wasn't going to wear these *together*. Is that what you thought? That's funny. Ha, ha, ha, ha, ha. No, what I was doing was, I was just showing you Clothing That I Own Currently. These are Currently In My Possession, these two items. That's what this is: an inventory reminder for *you*. I'll take them off now that you've been reminded."

I don't even try to do it myself anymore.

"Honey, what do you think? A striped shirt and a solid tie, or a solid shirt and pair of mukluks—what do you think? Help me out. A Beatle wig and a grass skirt, or maybe a goose-down vest and some sort of Viking helmet? Tell me, because I haven't used that part of my brain in several years. In fact, why don't you just choose something, lay it out, and I'll be in the crib until we have to leave."

Even if you're both dressed right, you're not leaving so fast. There's always something to keep you from where you're going.

Here's one: We're going out to rent a video—something, by the way, that couples in the 1700s never did. "Honey, after you fend off the British, pick up a tape for tonight. Something with Jack Lemmon."

I don't know when I'm going to learn that when you rent videotapes, it always ends up costing more than you thought it would. They have a big sign: "99 CENTS." You think, "It's a buck. It's nothing." So you'll get two, three. "We'll get five! It's just five bucks!"

Do you know how long it takes to watch five movies? A year and a half. You come back a year and half later and it costs you $1,400 to watch *Fried Green Tomatoes.* I simply refuse to learn.

Anyway, I'm dressed. I'm ready to go. My wife says, "Okay, I have to pee and put on my shoes. I just need two minutes."

Fine. So I start playing with the stereo—with the presumption that when she's ready, she'll say, "I'm ready," or something that will let me *know* she's ready, at which point I'll stop playing with the stereo, and we'll go.

Already I've presumed wrong.

A few minutes later, my bride comes back, ready to go, sees I'm still playing with the stereo, decides I'm not doing my share of "getting ready," and proceeds to busy herself with something else. She cleans a closet. Starts painting the garage. Something huge.

Now, I don't notice, because I'm playing. I'm happy. Twenty-five minutes later, she comes in, stands over me.

I sense bad mood. I say, "What—are you waiting for *me*?"

"Yes, I'm waiting for you. I've been ready for twenty-five minutes."

"Well, *I'm* ready. I've been ready since before you went upstairs to *get* ready. Why didn't you *say* you were ready?"

To which she says, "Let's just go."

We get in the car, we're not particularly talking. Feeling courageous, I open.

"Why would you start cleaning a closet when you know I'm ready and all you have to do is let me *know* that you're ready?"

She thinks really hard and comes up with, "Because I want you to take some responsibility."

I take a nice deep breath. I say nothing. But I'm thinking, "This really shouldn't be this hard. Before I was married, I never argued with *myself* about these types of things."

My choices are: (A) Get out of the car and live by myself, or (B) Push through this swamp and figure out what the hell we're talking about.

I go with Choice B, because, frankly, I really like the way her hair smells, and I know I would miss that.

"Okay," I venture. "Responsibility for *what*?"

She says, "For getting us out. It shouldn't be just *me*. I don't want to be the policeman here."

"How are you the policeman?"

"I don't know. I just always feel like the policeman and I don't like it."

You see, this is something you couldn't possibly know going in: this woman hates feeling like a policeman. I didn't even know that was a category of things that could go bad in a relationship: "Feeling-Too-Much-Like-Uniformed-Civil-Servants." You can only learn this on the job. (And again—this may only be an issue if you marry *my* wife, which, frankly, what are the chances of that?)

So we drive and we talk it out, and in short order, the smoke has cleared and she feels much better. I, by contrast, have a pounding in my eye that won't go away, and a huge, slow burning, festering resentment.

"ARE YOU KIDDING ME? I don't take responsibility? That's so not true. I really hate that kind of comment—like I'm constantly *auditioning*."

She's calm now. "How are you auditioning?"

"BECAUSE. What did you—just MEET me? You KNOW I take responsibility. And ANOTHER thing . . ."

And now *I* get to be nutty for a few miles.

It turns out, I have a thing about "Auditioning" that makes even less sense than her "Policeman" thing.

But the beauty part is, in any couple only one person

has to be sane at a time. You talk them out of *their* tree, so they can be coherent enough to talk you out of *your* tree. So ultimately, all the time you spend trying to understand the other person isn't even for their sake. You just want to make sure they're ready to handle *your* next psychotic episode.

Which proves what I've always suspected: Marriage is just an elaborate game that allows two selfish people to periodically feel that they're *not*.

The
Selfish
Monster

The great thing about being selfish and self-centered is you can do it anywhere, with anybody. It's not restricted to those you love. And it's not just me. Everyone is self-centered. But I'm really only concerned about *myself* here.

I know, for example, that I'm selfish when I *drive*.

The True Ugliness that lurks in our souls doesn't always come out, but in traffic, it comes out plenty.

When you're stuck in traffic, you hate everybody. "Oh, look at this idiot. Why doesn't he just GO? He sees I'm here, doesn't he? Why wouldn't he go? Come on, go go go go *GO!* If you would just go, there wouldn't *be* traffic. That's why there's traffic: your failure to go!"

We've got places to be and we want to be there *NOW.* It doesn't matter where. You could be on your way to the dentist to get raw nerves sucked out of your jaw, and you'd still be upset. "Hey, I'm going to miss the whole nerve-sucking thing. Come ONNNNN."

It's the guy directly in front of you you really hate. Somehow this is *his* fault. "If *he* would go, they'd *all* go. . . . Come ONNNNNNNN!"

And you obsess about this guy. You've been staring at the back of his head so long, you want to *be* him. "If I could be where he is, I would be so happy. Let me be in front of *him.* That's all I want. If I could just be where he is now, I would never ask for anything again, I swear."

Of course when you get to where he is, you're still not happy. "Look where he is *now,* the lucky sonovabitch. He's still doing better than me. All these people are looking back and laughing at me, I know it."

The only way to feel better is to turn around and look at the people behind *you.* "Yeah, well at least I'm ahead of *those* losers." We just want to be better off than somebody.

The only time we're nice on the road is if an ambulance has to get through. Suddenly everyone cooperates. People you've been cursing at and giving the finger to are suddenly your good friends. You put away your differences, and peace and harmony prevail as you clear a path for your neighbors in need.

Then, it's a mad rush for the Ambulance Wake. Everybody wants to get behind that ambulance. "I saw it first, buddy. I pulled over first, so I get to go ahead of you —that's how it works."

It's the Selfish Monster.

Ever been stuck behind an accident, and when you finally see the wreckage, you're actually *happy*? "Here we go, here's the problem. Things should pick up now, soon as we pass this carnage."

And when you tell your friends about it later, it's all about *you*.

"Sorry I'm late, some guy's car exploded. *Right in front of me.* Can you believe my luck? Lost a good fifteen minutes."

Sometimes, I must admit, I *become* the very people that I hate. I get distracted and kind of forget to drive. I'll sit at a green light for eight minutes because I forgot to look up. I'll slow down to twenty miles an hour because I forgot to press down my foot. This is less dangerous than driving fast and reckless, but actually more annoying to those in the car with you.

"Are you going to go around this guy or what?"

"He's going to go, relax. . . ."

"There's no driver. It's an abandoned car."

"Oh . . . I knew that."

Driving with your loved one can strain the relationship because, though you're doing it together, only one person's in charge. The passenger is your prisoner.

"Do you want *me* to drive?"

"No. Why?"

"Because I don't like the way you're driving."

"How am I driving?"

"I don't know, but you're making me crazy."

"*You* want to drive?"

"Yes."

"Too bad, *I'm* driving."

It's not like fighting over the TV clicker, where if the battle for control gets ugly, one of you can leave the room. Here, the doors are locked and you're doing sixty. Nobody's going anywhere. (Which is essentially Marriage, but with High-Speed Motion thrown in to make it interesting.)

If you're ever on a long car trip together, you find you start to recognize the cars and drivers around you. You start to judge them, like you know them.

"Look at that guy in the Mitsubishi—he's still smoking. He really should cut down. . . . I'm going to talk to him next time we stop."

"That lady in the RV. That's her fourth donut. How does she do that? Does she not *know* what she looks like?"

Sometimes if you're stuck in traffic with the same people, mile after mile, they genuinely become your neighbors. These are the people you turn to for solace. You complain to each other. First, you make eye contact. Then, little sympathetic sighs and dismissive waves of disgust.

"Ahhhhhhh, pppfffhhh." (I don't believe I've ever spelled that out before.)

Once in a while, you even roll down the window and chat. "Hey, can you believe this?"

"Well, *this* sucks, doesn't it? How is it over in your lane? Sucks?"

"Here, too. Sucks. Guess it sucks everywhere, huh?"

You develop a relationship with these people. Which is why I get upset when somebody tries to pass. It's like they're breaking up the relationship.

Your first response? You're shocked. You didn't see this coming. "What do you mean you're leaving? Why? Where are you going? I thought we all agreed we'd stick it out together. . . . What is it—you want to see other cars?

Is that it? I guess you need some *space* of your own, huh? Well, fine. Go. . . . Just *go*."

And the great moment of revenge: Two minutes later, they come crawling back. They want back in. But, of course, you don't let them in. You've been hurt, scorned— make them sweat.

"Hey, look who's back. I guess life in the fast lane didn't work out like you planned. Suddenly I'm looking good to you, huh? Well, get in line, baby."

Negotiating in Good Faith

———————A lot of times, the things you
do when you're alone aren't necessarily selfish, they're just
dopey. But you don't realize it till you see them bouncing
off someone else.

Actually, *everything* you do when you're alone looks
dumb. Ever watch what you do when you walk into the
house by yourself? There's no rhyme or reason to your
actions. Just ten minutes of random, halfhearted, ineffi-
cient activity.

You put down the mail and stand still. For about a
minute. You just stand there and stare at a chair. Then you
take your jacket off, not even all the way. Halfway off, so
your arms are still dangling. You open one piece of mail

and then get bored. You pop on the TV, flip through a few channels, looking for nothing at all in particular, and then forty seconds later, you shut it off. You weren't even *watching* TV. You just wanted to have it on. Sort of making sure the appliance works.

Then you open the refrigerator, stare at the shelves. Smell milk, put it back. Eat half a banana, read six words in a magazine, look out the window for two minutes. . . . No sense of purpose. Just lost in your own home. But no one sees, so no one knows.

However, when you live with another person, you become self-conscious. I find I do the same things, but I *announce* them. Gives the impression I've thought this through.

"I'm going to watch TV for a while."

"How long?"

"Fifteen seconds. Then I have to be at the window; I'm going to stare at the house across the street for a little while."

"How long?"

"Not more than ten seconds, because I have to eat half a banana and stare at a chair. And I'm already running late."

When two people live in one place, their individual habits get amplified.

For example: I'm not lazy. But I don't like to *move* a whole lot. I mean, if I'm doing something, I'll do it. I'm as active as the next guy. But if I'm sitting, I don't like to get up. Even if I'm facing the wrong way.

If I'm talking to someone whose chair isn't quite facing me, I'll talk to the side of their head. If I sit down and realize the TV is angled wrong, I won't get up to adjust. I'll watch it like that. I'll sit there and wait till someone walks by and ask *them* to move the TV.

Sometimes I may notice I'm sitting on something uncomfortable. I don't care. Like a stack of mail or something? It doesn't bother me. Certainly not enough to move.

I'm a big fan of Sitting.

I'll watch a show I'm not enjoying for 30, 40 minutes because I don't feel like looking for the remote control. Forget about getting up to actually, physically change the channel on the TV itself—that stopped years ago.

Once, we were watching TV and couldn't find the remote control. (I should preface this by saying I was really, really tired.)

Now, I sensed I was sitting on something hard that may very well have *been* the remote control, but I didn't have the energy to get up and confirm. (How sad is *that*? I didn't even have the drive to lean to one side. Even if just to dislodge an irritating piece of hardware from my person. Couldn't do it.)

Finally, my wife forcibly shoves me to one side and we find not only the remote control, but a pair of scissors, a glove she was looking all over for, and a tangerine.

I realized I am either (A) really, really, remarkably lazy, or (B) I have no sensory receptors in my left buttock. Either way, it might be a problem.

And once again, this kind of behavior is perfectly fine—*unless* you live with another human being. By yourself, who are you bothering? No one. In fact, it could even be an attribute. Nothing bothers you. You're a guy who's just okay with everything the way it is. But put someone else into the picture—now you're bothering *them.*

"Have you seen the new *People* magazine?"

"No."

"You didn't see it? It was right there, on the couch."

"I didn't see it."

"Are you sitting on it?"

"No."

"Get up."

"Really?"

"For one second."

I get up.

"Ha, I told you you were sitting on it."

"Well, look at that. . . . Hey, when did we buy tangerines?"

See, when someone else is involved, laziness doesn't look like Laziness. It looks like Indifference, Presumption, Insensitivity, Hostility—a whole rainbow of things that all sound worse than what it really is—Sitting There Minding Your Own Business.

Like dishes.

If I leave dishes in the sink, my wife *assumes* that *I* assume I can just leave them there for *her*. Not true. I assume nothing. I'll clean them—as soon as I notice them. Or as soon as they bother me.

Unfortunately, as I've mentioned, some things don't bother me right away. My wife gets bothered *sooner*. It's all a matter of timing. Learning each other's Lag Time; how long you have between Event and Annoyance of Said Event.

For example, if I use the jar of mustard at nine o'clock, I may not notice that it's still sitting on the counter until, oh, say—that Friday.

Now, if my wife notices sooner, does that make me insensitive? I think not. It's just who we are.

I would argue that if it bothers *you,* and *you* need to put it away, then by all means, put it away. I'm willing to let you do that. I will forgo my own schedule, so that *you* may honor *yours.* I will not be offended. Just don't *you* be offended and assume *I* assume, because you're assuming wrong.

I'm just Sitting Here Minding My Own Business.

The problem is, when two people live together, there is no more Business of Your Own. Your Own Business is closed. You've merged and gone public. You have to run everything by the partners. And if there are too many conflicts of interest, the business may go under, freeing the partners to once again open up smaller concerns by themselves.

Like all businesses, couples engage in endless meetings to discuss areas of management concern and division of labor.

"You know, we really should call the post office and tell them to hold our mail while we're away."

"*We?* You mean *me,* don't you?"

"No, I mean *we.* I didn't say 'you.' I said '*we.*' You *or* me."

"Oh really? Are *you* going to ever call the post office?"

A moment to think. "No."

"Then you mean 'me,' don't you?"

"Yeah."

Sometimes it works out well, and certain household responsibilities fall naturally to those who like doing them.

For example, my wife likes to pack suitcases, I like to unpack them.

My wife likes to buy groceries, I like to put them away. I do. I like the handling and discovering, and the location assignments.

"Cans—over there. Fruit—over there. Bananas—not so fast. You go over here. When you learn to not go bad so quickly, then you can stay with the rest of your friends."

There are things that nobody really *likes,* but one of you hates more than the other person does.

For example, someone has to take out the dog in the morning. Now, no one *wants* to get out of bed. But if you understand my affection for Sitting, multiply it a couple of times and you can imagine my enthusiasm for Lying Down. If I'm lying down, I really like to stay there.

So this particular task falls, by default, to my wife.

But there is actually a more complex negotiation at play here. You see, sometimes our beloved dog doesn't actually make it through the night. We occasionally wake up to find things on top of our carpets that hours earlier were *inside* our dog. I don't enjoy cleaning this up. But my wife *hates* it. I mean, she really hates it. She would rather not continue her life than be involved with this.

One morning, our dog was sick and left a particularly repulsive souvenir at the foot of the bed—a combination of grass, raspberry yogurt, and liner notes to a Ray Charles album. My wife, in a pathetically desperate last-minute plea bargain, blurted out, "I will take him out every morning for the rest of our lives if you clean up whenever he does *this*."

Sold.

Being a man who knows a good deal when he sees one, I jumped up, shook hands, and started cleaning up. After all, the dog only messes up the house once in a while, but he has to be taken out *every morning*. I thought it was a very sound investment.

It was only later, while I was straining dog puke from a sponge, that it hit me: if I'm in charge of cleaning up future In-House Accidents, there's no real incentive for my wife to rush the dog *out* of the house every morning. It's not her problem. So once again, ladies and gentlemen, you see how even when negotiating in the best of faith with someone you love, you can get badly, badly burned.

Alone

Together

———————————— Theoretically, marriage is all about Two people becoming as One. But in the real world —and let's be really clear about this—you ain't One. You're Two. And there's only so much two people can blend.

Like in bed. For all the advantages of sleeping next to another person, it's not always easy to figure out where everything goes. Arms and legs that didn't bother you all day are suddenly a burden.

Many people opt to minimize their Limb Placement decisions by sleeping on their own side of the Team Bed, an approach known as "Individual Free-Style Sleep." But even here there are choices to be made.

I myself am a big fan of the popular "One Arm Across Your Forehead, the Other Hand Resting Nicely on Your Groin." (Nine out of ten men sleep with at least one hand guarding their crotch. Not that this really protects anything, but if anyone tries to attack or pilfer, you're at least notified, and have a shot at dissuading them.)

But the real challenge is when you have *four* arms and legs to find homes for. Not so easy.

You got your "*Her* Head on His Chest, *His* Arm Around Her Shoulder" model, noted for its easy-access Chest Hair Fondling; there's the "Face Each Other and One of You Wrap Your Upper Leg Around the Other One's Legs," or the easy-to-remember "Lie There on Top of Each Other Supporting Your Partner's Body Weight With Your Own Rib Cage," which again—effective for conversation but not really suited for lengthy, sleep-oriented couplings.

For sleep, of course, you have your classic "Spoon" and "Reverse Spoon," both enjoyable, but tough ones in terms of breathing. One of you will suffocate, and I've always believed there's no point in being cozy if you're dead.

Then you've got the Thermal Levels to contend with. Not only are two people in the same bed never the same temperature, they're not even close. One is *freezing* and the other is *boiling*. There's no middle range. And you're both upset that your partner doesn't see it your way. "How can you be cold? I'm sweating rain forests here. . . . Come on, be like me. Be hot." The contention being that if the other person is uncomfortable, they should at least be uncomfortable in the same thermal direction as you.

But the real work of two people blending—the behavior stuff—is where things really get interesting. Because after so many years of being by yourselves, no matter how much "Us" paint you throw on top of it, the old "You" still shows through. And that's usually not a good thing.

A lot of guys think the highest compliment they can pay a woman is to treat her like "one of the guys." The whole "Treat others as you would be treated yourself" rule becomes "Treat others as if you were *by* yourself." They figure, "Surely we're beyond the silly formalities, the need to be civil. Let's relax. Be ourselves." And the women are thinking, "Let's *not*." Because they know where this leads.

"Hey!"

"What?"

"Did you just fart on my arm?"

"Sorry. I didn't know you were there."

See, when you're by yourself, you apply your own standards. It doesn't bother your Self that you stand in the middle of the room, drink 32 ounces of club soda, and belch out everything you've eaten since the Spring. Your Self may not care. Others, however, may.

And if you're with another person all the time, every repugnant component of your life must, by definition, happen in front of the other person. There's nowhere to hide.

So you learn to accept each other. Your best behavior is now and forever reserved for *outside* the house, and once you're inside, you're free to be the repellent American you really are. There's a tacit understanding. "I know all about *you,* you know all about *me,* and it'll all be our little secret."

You become a little team. It's the "two of you" against "everybody else." And you look out for each other. Your partner becomes the one person in the world you can go over to and say, "Do I have anything in my nose?"

That's your mutual job: protect your Ugly Truths from everyone but each other. Which is kind of nice, actually. Here is someone who will not only be honest with you, but whose love for you is so great it can withstand looking up your nose. Then they go right back to loving you like it never happened.

It's ironic that Everybody Else—to whom you owe nothing—is spared having to see what's in your nose. As if *they* deserve better. But your partner, the very person you love more than all others, gets to look right in there and investigate personally. That's *their* little privilege. One of the many bonuses for signing on for the long haul.

Don't Look at Me, I Just Live Here

────────────────────W hen you decide to share a home with another person, a lot of thought goes into finding the specific home you intend to share.

When my bride first moved into my apartment, it didn't work for either of us. *She* felt she was getting, at best, half of a place, and *I,* who was doing fine by myself, thought, "Hey, what happened to the other half of my place?"

It turns out, a house is like a bed: When you're getting along, it doesn't matter how small it is; and if you're *not,* all the elbow room in the world ain't going to help you.

But still, you're sure that somewhere out there your Dream House awaits.

A lot of times, when you go to look at a potential home, there are people living there. It's still *their* home. And I love walking into a place that already has Food Smells going. Those soupy, cakey, meaty smells. I don't even want the food, I just want the smell.

They should make a *spray* for people who don't cook: An aerosol can that, for seven bucks, makes the whole place smell like pot roast. Or you could have a fumigator guy come in every three months.

Doorbell rings. "Who is it?"

"Pot roast man!" And he sprays around the house.

"You want me to spray the bathroom?"

"No, that's okay."

"How about under the sink?"

"Okay, maybe just coffee and cake."

It's hard to reject a house without feeling like you're rejecting the people who live there; these nice people who are eating dinner while you investigate every nook and cranny of their home. You walk around the house, look in their closets, touch all their things, then look them in the eye and say, "You know what? *No.*" And walk away.

In essence, "This house is good enough for *you,* but we're gonna try to beat it."

It's hard. And you always walk through the place imagining a life that has nothing to do with reality. Planning things you'll never do: parties and soirées with tantalizing guests and performers from other lands. "This is great. We can have a dance floor *here,* a cocktail area *there,* the orchestra can set up near the receiving line . . ."

And then you move in and spend the rest of your life eating corn chips out of a bowl in front of the TV.

"What happened to the dancing and the waltzing and jugglers and cocktail pavilion?"

"I thought we were someone else. My mistake."

Because in real life, you're always in one of three places: the kitchen, the bathroom, or the bedroom. There are only three things to do in life, and that's where we do them.

W hen you actually move into a house, you learn quite quickly how little you know about *anything.*

Day One, the guy comes to turn on the electricity. He asks me one question:

"Excuse me, where is your main power supply?"

Right there, I was stumped. First question as a homeowner, I had nothing.

"I don't know. It's probably outside. Did you look

outside, because I think I saw it there earlier. . . . Okay, I'm going to level with you, sir, I don't really know what a main power supply looks like. What is it? Is it a big thing? Maybe it's *inside*. It's definitely either inside or outside, I know that. Tell you what—why don't you *find* it, and that'll be your first little job. . . . *You* find it, I'll *have* it. That'll be what *I* do. You find it and do certain things with wires that I don't understand, and then I'll give you more money than you deserve. Is that fair?"

If you don't know what you're doing, you're at the mercy of anyone with a truck and a business card. And problems come up I never heard of.

We had this *snake* in the backyard. Not a big snake but big enough to make *me* pass out. So I called the guy, the snake guy. Snake Man. That was his name. "Snakes in the Yard? Call Snake Man." He had a truck with a little picture of a snake and everything. I said, "We have a snake."

He says, "Where?"

Once again, I say, "*Finding* it will be pretty much up to you. I'm just telling you we *have* one."

He looks around and then tells me, "Listen, the kind of snake you have there is fine. It's a *good* snake to have, because they scare away mice. You *want* these kind of snakes."

I say, "Okey-dokey." And I pay him. For doing nothing. I give the man forty-five dollars for allowing me to continue to have the snake I already had.

So now I rest comfortably in the knowledge that I have no mice, because the mice are all scared of my snake.

Then I remember, I'm scared of the snake, too. That's why I called the guy in the first place. Evidently, the only way I'm going to get rid of this snake is to scare him with something *bigger*. A mongoose. A cheetah. But then I'll have to scare *them* away, and it will never end. The animals will just get bigger and bigger. I'm going to end up with a *hippo* in the living room.

"Don't worry, honey—they scare away the bison. Did you notice there were no bison around? Why do you think that is? They're scared. Nice, huh? Hippo Man was here today, he explained the whole thing; forty-five bucks, we're bison-free for a year."

I believe whatever they say. I don't know who They are, but I trust them. And They say a lot of things.

"You know what They say: 'Cold hands, warm heart.' "

"Who says that?"

"I don't know."

"Hey, you know what they say about swimming on a full stomach. . . ."

"Who actually said that?"

"I don't know, but why would they lie?"

I just assume "They" know everything. "They" and "the Guy," as in "Ask the Guy, *he'll* know."

"I'm sure the Guy can fix it."

These are the two authorities running the whole show —They and the Guy. The Guy, I believe, is president of They.

"You should have the guy check out that noise."

"I *did*. I brought it to the guy—he said he couldn't fix it."

"The Guy couldn't fix it? Are you sure this guy is good?"

"That's what They say."

All my life, I called the Guy. And if you could *get* him, he'd come over and fix it. Now I own a house, and I *am* the Guy—which doesn't help anybody. I can *get* me; that's not a problem. I'm available as hell. It's knowing what to do when I *get there* that concerns me.

Usually I look at the problem and say, "Honey, call the Guy. I don't know *exactly* what's wrong here, but my gut tells me flooding in a bedroom is bad. It can't be right."

And I don't love *dealing* with the Guy when he

comes over. I'm much better at telling my *wife* how to deal with him.

"Look, honey, I gotta go, but when the cable guy gets here, make sure you tell him that we are *not* happy with the reception! Be firm with the guy. That was the problem last time, you weren't firm. *I* would do it myself, but I've got to go Gather and Hunt. I gotta go slay an elk. But if the guy shows up before I get back, for God's sake—BE FIRM WITH HIM."

Again, this is part of that delicate balance between Men and Women that allows us to be together. In fact, I think the whole reason men and women get together in the first place is because we each can do certain things, and if you get together, everything gets done. Whatever comes up, somebody's good at that.

Ever catch a sweater on a hook and get that thread that sticks out? Women have learned that's not a big deal. They know you can turn the sweater inside out, pull it through, tie a knot, and in twelve seconds you've got a new sweater. They got brochures as youngsters that explained this.

Men did not get this pamphlet. Men will stare at the rip for half an hour and whine. "Oh, look at that! Do you believe that? Brand-new sweater, too! Now I gotta throw it out. There's no way this can be saved."

On the other hand, women rarely get involved with connecting stereos, which is the one thing most men *can* do. Me, anyway.

And it works out well. I'll be putting up a set of speakers, and suddenly go, "Oh no—look what I just did to this sweater—caught it on the speaker!"

And instantly, we *both* have something to do.

Chicken
or
Fish

I can't believe how much of our life is spent planning food.

"What do you feel like eating?"

"I'm not really hungry."

"You gonna want to eat later?"

"Probably."

"So we should get something *now*."

"Nah, we'll get it later."

"*Later* everything'll be closed. Let's get something now."

"Alright, like what?"

"That's what I'm asking *you*."

And it never ends.

Since we got married, I don't think a day has passed that at least one conversation with my wife hasn't ended with the words "Um, I don't know . . . I guess . . . chicken."

Not one day. Do you understand this? Not one. The word "Chicken," preceded by some unenthusiastic whine of indifference and frequently followed by an even less enthusiastic "Or maybe *fish,* I-don't-care-it's-up-to-you," is by far the most commonly heard expression in our home. Perhaps second only to "*You* get it."

Chicken or fish. That's basically what it comes down to.

I wish we could just get pills to take the place of meals. Little full-balanced meals in pill form. Then you wouldn't have to decide, you wouldn't have to talk about it —huge chunks of your life would be freed up.

Though I'm sure in no time I'd be on the phone going, "What do you feel like tonight—Chicken Pill or Fish Pill?"

Here's the thing with decisions. I can *make* them. I just don't feel sure about them afterward.

A friend of mine said, "Always go with your gut."

Then another friend said to me, "You know what? You should listen to your heart."

So now I have one *more* choice to make: Do I go with my heart or my gut? I can't decide. I gotta do an entire autopsy. My heart says *yes,* my gut says *no,* my colon is iffy —I just don't know who to listen to.

Say we're in a coffee shop, I'm ordering breakfast, and the waitress says, "With those eggs, you want pancakes or waffles?"

Pancakes. Very easy. Firm, clear-cut decision.

She walks away, and immediately I realize I should have had the waffles. . . . Yup, waffles was the way to go. Look at that guy over there, *he* got the waffles, *he* looks very happy.

"Excuse me, sir, how're you enjoying those waffles? Pretty good, huh?"

Great. *He* got the waffles. He'll have a better breakfast, he'll have a better day, a better life. He'll go on to make a contribution to society, people will remember this guy for years. . . .

Me? I got the friggin' pancakes.

A lot of times, you're home and you're too hungry to even talk about food. So you stand over the sink and start eating whatever you have—celery and some assorted nuts from a gift basket you got three years ago. By the time you figure out what you're going to eat, you're bloated, queasy, and no longer interested in food.

Then there are things you don't even *realize* you ate. You're on the run all day, you grab what you can, and at the end of the day you realize—you're a goat. You've eaten whatever you saw, whenever you saw it. And somewhere in your belly lie pathetically odd combinations of foods:

"A quarter pound of hummus and some Cracker Jacks."

"Fifteen pieces of bread and a sour ball."

Foods that have no business being together.

"Chicken salad, blueberries, and a Mounds Bar."

And couples like to *report* what they had. They need to share. Like without this information, they'd be keeping secrets.

You come home: "You know what I had today? Milk. Milk and a half a cucumber. How do you like *that*?"

Like it's an accomplishment. You're proud that you can sustain your body weight despite a punishing nutritional intake.

Sometimes it's more of a confessional. You feel bad about what you ate, and you want to enlist the help of your partner in berating yourself.

"You know what I ate today? A bacon burger, M&Ms, and a thing of fried onions I found in the car."

"You're a bad person."

"That's what I thought—wanted to make sure."

But someone always gets hurt in these conversations.

"I had a bowl of cereal and two fat-free cookies."

"Is that good or bad?"

"I can't believe I ate so much."

"But the cookies were fat-free."

"Yeah, but I ate *two*."

"Well, you look great."

"I'm stuffed."

"So we won't eat anything tonight."

"Don't tell me what I can eat."

With someone you love, food becomes politics.

We're in a restaurant and I'm about to eat a big fried piece of something crusty, and my loved one, very discreetly, gives me the little "Do you really want that?" look. I think, "She's probably right." And I pass.

Later—during the *same meal,* she orders some Chocolate Sticky Pie of Death, and I, in the most loving tone I can muster, step into the ring with "Sweetie, are you going to be upset later if you eat that?"

She looks at me for a long time, tells the waiter to go away, and then flings one of those really big spoons at my throat.

I say, "Hey, wait a minute, you said the same thing to me."

She says, "Yeah, 'cause *you* don't mind."

"Right, because you said it out of Love. Out of Concern."

"That's right."

"So, if I say the same thing to *you,* wouldn't you naturally assume that I—"

"It's different."

"Why?"

"Because *I* mind."

You see how it works? There are different eating rules for each of you. But, again, you don't know what they are until you've broken them.

We're out for dinner, the food comes, and I jump in. I grab the pepper thing and put some pepper on the food. I start eating.

And I notice I'm getting the look. I've done something wrong. I look up. "What?"

She skips the specific and goes straight to the general. Very sweetly: "Let me make it easy for you: If you ever have something, anything at all, please see if I'd like some."

I said, "Did you want pepper?"

She goes, "No, but I might."

"But you didn't actually want—"

"It would be nice of you to think of *me.*"

"Okay, I understand that, but just to clarify about the pepper—you don't want any."

"No, thanks."

"You're not interested in pepper."

"Not this time."

See? We were just setting the rules for next time.

Sometimes you have to make up rules as you go along.

Example:

My bride is trying to not eat meat. I try to be supportive.

"Do you want me to *not* eat this chicken in front of you?"

"No, no, it's fine."

" 'Cause I don't want you to be tempted and then eat it and feel bad about it."

"I won't."

"And I don't want you to make *me* feel bad about eating meat."

"No, no, I won't."

"You sure?"

"Yeah, I'm fine. Eat the chicken."

Fine. So I'm eating the chicken, and I notice she keeps watching me eat.

I say, "What?"

She picks up my plate and with a real sad face says to my food, "I'm sorry people eat you, Mr. Chicken."

"Hey!"

"What?" she says.

I say, "Don't do that."

"Do *what*?"

I had to think for a second, then came up with, "Don't apologize to my food while I'm eating it."

Isn't that sad? That was the best rule I could think of. In case it ever came up again, and we needed to refer to a mutually agreed upon bylaw, I decreed that from that point forth, "Thou shalt not apologize to my food while I'm eating it."

That should pretty much cover it. With, of course, the universally accepted *sub*-clause: "And don't call my food 'Mister.'"

How

Are

You?

_____ I just cleaned out my address book.

My wife pointed out I had names in there I haven't called since third grade. People who've moved off the continent, couples who have divorced, some remarried, and a few names that, frankly, I don't even know who they are. There was one entry that just said, "Rusty." And next to it, "Call after five." For the life of me, I have no idea what this means.

Certain letters in every address book fill up right away. "M" and "S," for example. Very popular letters. There's no room. You can't get anyone new in there— there's a waiting list of three, four years. If I meet someone whose name begins with "M" or an "S," I tell them right up front that we can't be friends. I just don't have the room.

Whereas "X," "Q," and "Z"—I can move you in today. I've got nothing but space. And I'm dying to use those pages. My dream is to meet the Xylophone family and fill that section right up.

There's something very satisfying about starting a new address book. It's like a new calendar: all fresh, clean, and full of boundless potential.

I've noticed that as I get older, I buy *next* year's calendar earlier and earlier. There seem to be more Things to Do, and we need more time to plan them.

When you're a kid, you don't have this problem—you've got nothing to do. You can buy a calendar in March, April—there's no real rush. You remember your first calendar? One appointment: "See that? That's my birthday. Otherwise, I'm free. I'm absolutely open till the fifteenth."

But the older you get, the harder it seems to be to make the simplest of plans. I bumped into a friend of mine running out of an elevator the other day.

"Hey, how ya doin'? Everything good? You're good? Family is good? Kids are good? Good. I'm good, everything is good."

We just bombarded each other with "goods." "Everything's good? Good. I'm good, you're good. It's good we're all good." There's no time for details, just headlines. "Anybody we know of die? No? Good. So everybody's good? Good."

Some people actually *tell* you how they are, and you might not want to know.

"How are you, good?"

"Actually, I'm just getting over an intestinal virus. . . ."

"Oh my, look at the time! I thought I could squeeze in a flu story, but it turns out, I can not."

It's not that we don't care about our friends. We care, we just don't always know what we're supposed to say.

"How's everything, good?"

"I just lost my job."

"Ohhh . . ." You stand there a little while. Silence. Then try and pick things up.

"But everything *else* is good? Family? How's the family? Everybody good?"

"They're all sick."

"Really. . . ." Check your watch, try again.

"But *you* seem healthy. Physically, how're you doing? You doing good?"

"Three weeks to live."

"Alrighty. . . ." Then you put down your bags, 'cause you're in for a while.

With some people, you can tell by the way they *ask* that they don't really care. Listen to how they say, "How are you?" They don't really say, "How are you?" They say, "How *are* ya?" Not the same. They hit the "are" and shortchange the "ya." "How *are* ya . . . how *are* ya?"

Do you understand the difference?

"How are *you*?" is good.

It's all about *you*. *"How are YOU?* I'm interested in specifically *you*. Out of all the people in the world, how is it to be *you*? That's what concerns me primarily—how *you* are."

"How *are* ya?" is not the same thing.

"How *are* ya?" means "Just say 'good,' and walk away. I don't really want to know. Register that I asked, then proceed not to tell me."

And sometimes people assign you to be greetings messenger. I don't pass on greetings when people tell me to. I don't need the pressure.

You see a friend, they say, "When you see Alan, tell him I said, 'Hi.' "

Right, sure.

Problem is, if you say, "Hi" to Alan, he goes, "Oh, you saw Joel? Tell him I said, 'Hi.' How is he doing?"

Now I've got to run back to Joel, "Alan told me to tell you 'Hi' and wants to know how you're doing?"

"Oh, did you see him? How's *he* doing?"

Why don't the two of *you* get together and leave me out of it? I have things to do.

But my friend and I did promise to get together.

So, he calls me, and the first thing we have to decide is what *meal* we're talking about. Socializing invariably involves food, and often, a bona fide meal. Because you need the focal point. You can't just walk back and forth between two trees and chat. How would you know when you're finished? That's why you need food.

At least a hot beverage and a muffin. This way, if the conversation drags, you have something to talk about. "Ooh, that's good coffee." (Which offers more potential than "Boy, look how far apart those two trees are.")

Sometimes your days get so busy, you have no actual meal open. Breakfast, lunch, and dinner are taken, so you go for quasi-meals.

"How about drinks at five?"

If that doesn't work, you have to start making up *new* meals.

"We'll have peanuts at noon."

"Corn chips at three."

Unfortunately, this is another case where you have to let some friends go.

"It's not that I don't like you, it's just that there are no more food groups left. We could do Oysterettes at three-thirty, but what's the point, really?"

That's what's great about Coffee.

It's the only meal for which the name of the food is also the official name of the event. "Coffee." "We'll get together for Coffee." We know what we're doing, and we know what we'll be having: coffee.

Makes it simple when you get there.

"Do you want to look at a menu?"

"No, I already know: coffee. That's why we got together. We got together for—Coffee. That's what we discussed, that's what I'll be having."

It's the only food that has that advantage. You never say, "Let's get together for lamb."

"I'm in town, let's get together for Fresca."

"Whattya say? Grapes for everyone."

You never hear it. It's just not the same draw as Coffee.

I love coffee. I don't *drink* coffee, but I love it. I drink tea, and I don't like it. That's my life in a nutshell, ladies and gentlemen, I consistently drink a hot beverage I don't enjoy.

Let me say something about tea. Tea starts bad and never gets better. You put in honey, cream, sugar, lemon, and you still go, "Ooh, that's bad!"

And the people who *make* tea know it's bad. That's why they give you so many choices. You go into a store, there's a thousand types of teas. Every herb, fruit, and spice in every combination. They're desperate to make this stuff palatable.

And it almost works. You think, "Wow! Look at this! Apple Cinnamon Mango Cherry tea. This should be good. I like all of those things. This is going to be just great."

You take a sip and go, "Nope. That's still very bad." I don't know how they go wrong with that, but they do.

So, when a waitress asks, "How would you like your tea?" I already know.

"I won't." Right off the bat. "I won't enjoy it, but it's not your fault. Just bring me hot liquid and a muffin, so I can talk to my friend here."

The greatest social food of all time is Chinese food. The whole purpose of this particular cuisine is to *share*. You get lots of different things, put them in the middle of the table, and you all share. But I find, even with people I like, I can't stop taking inventory.

I'm smiling, but I'm thinking, "How many shrimps

has *he* had so far? This fat bastard's got fourteen shrimps on his plate—two on his fork, three in his mouth that he didn't even chew yet; that's like nineteen shrimps. *I've* got three hundred snow peas and a dead noodle. . . . I can't even get a fork in there. The man is like a windmill."

And when couples go out socially, they're no longer people. They're *couples*. And couples don't talk like regular people.

They become *teams*. Little tag-team storytelling teams. She starts, *you* finish, you start, *she* finishes. You correct each other, interrupt each other, and no one knows exactly who they should be listening to.

Ever been out with four or five couples? It's like the Conversation Olympics. Whatever subjects come up, every couple has to compete.

"We had an experience like that, too." Then you step forward and tell *your* piteous little tale, and the conversation moves clockwise around the table, everybody telling *their* version of essentially the same story.

By the time it gets to the semifinals, it gets very tough. *Your* story has to be more interesting than the last couple. If Couple Number One lost their luggage in Mexico, Couple Two lost their luggage *and their passports*.

Couple Three has to beat that. "We lost our luggage, our passports, and our . . . *house* was stolen, too. And our children! The whole family, everything. We called American Express and we got new kids the next day . . . two girls and a boy, so it worked out well—but for a while there, we were *quite* alarmed."

Sometimes your team *has* no story. You have to huddle frantically with your partner: "Honey, Honey, quick—do we have anything like that? Airport, luggage—anything? Remember you lost that comb that time? Is there anything in that? . . . Come on, hurry up, we're next. THINK, man, THINK. Okay, we're up." Big smile. "Yes, we had the same thing happen to us . . . this was three years ago. . . ." And you're off and running.

Sometimes you're in the middle of your story, you look around the table, and you realize—nobody's listening. They're talking amongst themselves, paying the check . . . And you're thinking, "Am I the dullest person in the world? What happened here?"

And then, the saddest moment in the world: You look at your wife and discover *she's* listening. She, who's heard the story a thousand times. But, God bless her, she doesn't have the heart to let your story plummet like a boulder. So she sits there pretending she's interested. And what's even more pathetic is *you continue to tell her.* You don't want to stop.

"You know, *we* once . . . anyone listening? You

know, *we* once had a thing . . . in Florida, actually . . . We were in Florida"—and you turn right to your wife— "Honey, remember in Florida, that time? The cabdriver at the airport . . ."

And finally she leans in discreetly and says, "You can stop now, nobody's listening. You don't have to amuse me."

"But I was trying to amuse *them*."

"But they're not listening."

"I listened to *their* stories."

"I know, honey, I know . . ."

When you've been together long enough, you know each other's stories. That's why a lot of times you see couples in their eighties sitting and not talking: They've heard everything. They know. "When we got married, I told you everything I had done up to that point. And since then, *you were there*. What could I possibly tell you? . . . What happens if we *don't* talk? Can we try that? Could we just *read*? And if we read something interesting, we'll talk about that. Whaddya say?"

People who get married later in life have that great advantage. "Hey, baby, I've got stories till we die. Things I haven't even *hinted* to you about. Did you know I went to junior high school with FDR? That's right. Sweet fella. I was going to tell you later."

Tonight We'll See a Movie, Tomorrow We'll Kiss

It just so happens that in life there are the exact same number of people who like olives as people who don't. And they usually end up together.

No one knows how this works.

But next time you're in a restaurant, look around. Someone who can't stand olives will accidentally *get* some, and the person they're with will say, "I can't believe you don't like olives," and happily eat their olives.

See, a lot of things are that much simpler when you're a couple. Like ordering food. Couples develop their own strategies.

"Here's what we do. I got it, I got it—I *got* it. . . .

Here's the plan. *I'll* get the chicken, and *you* get the salmon, and that way we're covered."

That's another big plus about being Two instead of One. There are *two* dishes, so if one of you makes a mistake, there's always Backup Fish.

"I'll get the chicken, and then, if it stinks, I'll eat your salmon. . . . What? If *yours* stinks? Well, then you got a problem, 'cause mine turned out pretty good. Hey, nobody told you to order bad. Live and learn."

Going to a movie is easier, too. Couples are good at this because you can split up the responsibilities.

"Honey, I'm gonna park the car, you get out and buy the tickets—I'll meet you on line." Everybody has a job.

It's a military operation, and the two of you are a precision drill team.

"Okay. You get on the ticket *buyers'* line. I will park the car, come around the northwest corner, and get on the ticket *holders'* line. I'm at the ticket holders', you're at the ticket buyers'. Now, at nineteen hundred hours, the doors will open, and I'll have to move out. My regiment's leaving. If I don't have tickets in hand, we're dead. Get me those tickets. Now cover me—I'm going in!"

Of course, this type of expertise doesn't happen overnight; it takes months and months of Saturday nights to practice. You must each accept that there is a job to be done and sacrifices to be made. There's no romance involved; it's all business. "Tonight we'll see a movie, tomorrow we'll kiss. Now get out of the car and go go go go GO!"

Couples just starting out don't know this. Ever see first-date couples at a weekend movie? No. Because they never get in.

They haven't developed this taste for blood. They're too busy holding hands, being polite. "Which movie would you rather see? Because if you'd rather see something else . . . Oh, look—everything seems to be sold out."

Of course it's sold out! It's Saturday, eight o'clock. Separate! Split up! Do your jobs, be nice to each other afterward.

Even when you get *into* the theater, it's not over. You have to get seats. Now, again, there's a science to this.

You walk into the theater, grab the first two seats you see. Doesn't matter where they are, and you may very well not sit there. But grab them. That's your fallback position.

Now one of you guards the fallback position, while the other one goes to look for *better* seats. You set out in the jungle with a machete and a map, and periodically throw your gaze back to the fallback position, secure in the knowledge that, at worst, you've got two sucky seats in the back waiting for you.

To find better seats, you have to bother other people. You see a guy next to a jacket. "Excuse me, is that seat taken?" You have to ask. Because you don't know— Is he saving it? Is he dating his clothing? It's not always clear.

Sometimes you see a jacket *and* a hat—he's waiting for *two* friends. Once in a while you see a trail of clothing: jacket, hat, shoes, pants, socks, underwear, tie clip, belt— and way down at the end there's one guy sitting there naked and embarrassed. "Yes, they're *all* coming back. We're a group of twelve—I underdressed. I didn't think this through. Do you mind moving on? Please!"

And when you find your seats, it's *still* not over. One of you has to go back out to get the popcorn. That's usually my job. I'm happy to do it, but there's no moment more embarrassing than when you come back into that dark theater and realize you don't know where you're sitting. Suddenly, you're 4 years old and lost at the circus. You're near tears: "Honey? Honey—" You're sitting in people's laps: "Sorry, wrong row. . . . Honey, where are you? . . . I got the Gummi Bears you wanted. . . ."

If you can't find the seats, you've got to go to the front row and walk up the entire aisle, in plain view of everyone, hoping your partner will see you and come to your rescue. Of course, they're watching the movie at this point, and the last thing they're thinking about is *you*.

So you're wandering up and down the aisle like an idiot. "Help me . . . somebody . . . don't you see I'm dying here?" You're standing in front of a crowd with your arms full of crap *you* didn't even want. "Someone pull me out of this hell!"

You bump into other guys who are just as lost.

"Honey?!"

"Babe?!"

"Sweetheart?!"

"Hey, *my* wife is 'sweetheart.' "

"Sorry . . . HONEY?"

That's all you hear: men whining, and women whispering men's names loudly.

"Steve! Steve!"

"Leonard!"

"Mitchell! I'm over here!"

It's pathetic. In this situation, my advice is—sit next to *any* woman, it doesn't matter who. And just level with her. "Look, Mitchell is not coming back. I just saw him go into the wrong theater, so he won't be back for some time. My wife is sitting with a guy named Steve, Steve is with Leonard's wife—it's all screwed up. But I'm a guy, I got popcorn, it's the same exact thing. So just tell me what I missed. What happened so far?"

You watch the movie, and you settle up afterward.

There are other benefits to having a Permanent Partner.

Ever been invited somewhere you really don't want to go? If you're married, you always have someone else to *blame.*

"Next Saturday? You know, I'd love to, but I'm pretty sure my wife made plans. . . . Yeah, let me check with her and get back to you."

Of course, I try to weasel out of getting back to them, too.

"You know, honey, I really think *you* should call them. After all, they're *your* friends. . . . Alright, they're *my* friends, but you met them, didn't you? Well, there you go. Besides, they like you better. I'll tell you what. *I'll* dial and *you* talk to them. Is that fair? We'll split it 50-50."

Three weeks ago, my wife tells me we're going to a party for a woman she works with who is going to have a baby. I'm uneasy.

"What is this—like a *shower*?"

She says, "No, it's not a shower. It's a party."

"There going to be guys there?" I ask.

She says, "Yes, there'll be guys there."

Then it hit me: when did *this* happen? I spent the first big chunk of my life wondering if there were going to be *girls* there; now I'm checking to make sure there are *guys* there. Something has changed.

You see, single men judge social events solely by How Many Women Are Going to Be There. It's what they ask before they go, and what they talk about when they get back. No matter what the event. It could be a funeral. "Man, you should have seen this woman sitting behind the widow. Was she *gorgeous*."

It could be anything. A soccer riot. "I was pressed against this girl from Santiago you would not believe."

But now that I'm married and no longer looking to meet women, I want to make sure there are other married guys there, so I'm not the only one not meeting women.

In fact, it's not about *meeting* women. It's a matter of Balance. There's a Guy-to-Girl Ratio that makes us comfortable, and we're always checking that ratio.

That's why the minute somebody has a baby, that's the first question: "Boy or girl?" You need to know. We're keeping track. A perpetual, universal head count: how many boys, how many girls. "So, what'd they have—boy or a girl? Which is it? The Penis Model, or the Not-So-Much-A-Penis Model? Either one is great, I just need to know."

No wonder we're all so consumed with sex: from the second we're born, that's the first place everybody's looking. They pull you out: "Let's see what you got—specifically *there*."

They don't care if you have a head or a back, but

whatever is going on between your legs—they need to know *now*.

Anyway, we go to this friend's baby's party, and somehow *I* was responsible for getting the *card*.

How do you find the right card for someone you've never heard of?

What is the exact sentiment you're trying to express?

"I know nothing about you, but I'm sure you're a nice enough person."

"We hardly know you, what did you expect—cash?" You never see those kind of cards.

I love when they take a card and concoct every family / relationship combination imaginable: "From the Two of Us to the Two of You," "From the Three of Us to the Three of You," "From Some of Us to All of You," "From Both of Us to Nobody in Your Area . . ."

Then they break it up by occupations: "To a Wonderful Boss from a Terrific Secretary," "From a Belligerent Osteopath to a Nifty Teamster." Every job, every adjective.

I once went up to the guy at the register and said, "You know, a friend of mine just got a job on the same day as his anniversary, and his dog just had puppies, but sadly his grandfather passed away that afternoon. Is there a card that might cover the whole thing?"

He said, "Sure. From the whole family, or just your-self?"

So they have it. You just have to ask.

And let me just say this:

It *is* important that you get the *right* card. Don't get one that's *almost* right and try to change it by hand. People know when you do that, and they don't enjoy it. They mock you when you leave.

And don't pretend you don't know what I'm talking about, either. You want a "Dad" card, but they only have "Grandpa," so you think, "We'll cross out 'Grand' and make it 'Pa.' That'll work. . . . And, hey, everybody call him 'Pa,' so I don't look stupid. 'Hi, Pa,' 'How ya doing, Pa?' It'll be like 'Bonanza,' it'll be fun."

Or a little kid-card that you adjust for adults? "Today you're five, you're a big boy." Little flick of the pen: " 'Well, today you're *sixty*-five.' How do you like that? 'Today you're sixty-five, *boy-o-boy*.' We'll make the giraffe a set of golf clubs, he'll never know. His neck becomes a nine iron, and it's a little bag with hooves . . ."

This shower-that's-not-a-shower-just-a-party turns out to be a *surprise* party. Can someone please explain to me the appeal of the Surprise Party?

It's never worth the effort. You spend months planning, keeping secrets, avoiding people, lying, scheming, spreading misinformation—all so that when the guy walks in the room, you yell, "SURPRISE!" and he calmly goes, "Hmm, well I'll be darned."

That's it. Three seconds. Just so the guy can be darned. After the three seconds, you have the exact same party you would have had if the guy knew the whole time.

And if you're the surpris*ee,* it's even worse, because you have to spend the whole evening answering the same question: "Did you know? When did you know? You didn't know? Oh, come on, you knew. You had to know! When did you know?"

You have to convince them. "I didn't know. I *didn't.* I'm telling you, I didn't know. It's my party—stop grilling me."

Also, if you're the one being surprised, no one talks to you for three weeks before. They're afraid of blowing the surprise. So they don't call you, they won't get together with you, nothing. They avoid you like the plague.

Now you're depressed: you're getting older *and* you have no friends.

So you figure, "Fine. I'll spend my birthday alone. Who needs them?"

You walk in: "SURPRISE!!!" And now you've got to

spend an evening with two hundred people you're not talking to anymore.

A big party hazard for couples is Flirting. Everyone loves to do it, no one likes to be called on it.

Here's my thinking: The only reason people flirt is they want to know they still Have It. They don't necessarily want to do anything with it, but in case they ever do, it's good to know it's still there.

You're at a party, you're talking to someone, you're laughing, they're laughing . . . but what you're really thinking is:

"If I weren't married, and you weren't married, and no one ever knew what other people do, and actions had no consequences, and pretty much everything in the universe was different than it actually is—then something would actually happen here, wouldn't it? It would? I knew it! I just *knew* it. Alright—I'll see ya around. I just wanted to make sure."

Even if someone you *know* has an affair, you get hurt, because the discussion inevitably seeps over to *your* house.

"Isn't that unbelievable about Wendy and Michael?"

"Really."

"If that ever happened to *us,* would you leave me?"

"Yes."

"No, seriously."

"I *am* serious. I would kill you and then leave you."

The smart thing would be to drop it here. (But if you were really smart, you wouldn't have brought it up in the first place.)

"No kidding around, you would really leave me?"

"What is the POINT of this conversation?"

"No point . . . I would just hate to think that we couldn't survive a bump like that . . ."

"What bump?"

"No bump!"

"What are you saying?"

"I'm just saying . . . hypothetically."

"And why are you bringing this up *now*? Is there something you want to tell me?"

And there is *no* way out. You have to walk out of the house, go over to Wendy and Michael's house, and smack them because this whole thing is basically *their* fault.

The "Turn Around and Look"

Certain realities of marriage don't kick in right away. I was married six, seven months —happily married, *joyfully* married—and *still,* one day it just hit me: "I'm never going to be with any other woman naked, *ever*? Seriously? . . . In other words, out of all the different people, body types, shapes, and sizes, you're saying: These are the last breasts I'm ever gonna touch? Interesting. . . . I don't think I understood that."

It has to settle in. Bring it up again the next day. "Just to clarify . . . What you're saying is: These hands will not touch the skin of another woman for, literally, *ever*? No matter what? . . . Even if we're in different countries? Or we're mad at each other or something?

Uh-huh. . . . So, you're saying, basically, 'No.' . . . 'No' would be the word for me to hang on to here. . . . Geez. . . . And the same for *you*? I'm the last guy you're ever going to see naked? Wow. . . . well, good luck to *you*."

It's a mourning process you must go through together.

Because no matter how much in love two people are, you never lose sight of the fact that there are *other* people out there, too. And several of them are attractive. You can't help but notice this.

And this has nothing to do with Not Committing. It's easy to commit. The hard part is ruling out other commitments.

I learned this from my dog.

I'm eating potato chips; my dog comes over and stares at me with those doggy eyes.

"Can I have a potato chip, please?"

"No."

"Okay." He sits right there. Stares at me.

"Can I have a potato chip, please?"

As if we didn't just have this conversation.

"Come on, just give me one, I'll never bother you again."

"Alright, fine. Here."

Chomp!

"Could I try one more, please?"

"You said that was the last one."

"Well, I made a mistake. Can I have *that* one? The one going in your mouth? That's the one I *really* want."

"You sure this time?"

"Yes. That's the one that will satisfy my curiosity about *all* potato chips. I swear it this time."

It's not the potato chip he wants. He just wants to know he can have *another* potato chip afterward.

Maybe we're foolishly searching for something even more perfect.

Like when you're in a store, and you're ready to buy something, but you still ask the guy if there's anything "in the back."

"You don't have this a little bigger? A little smaller? More blue? Less blue?"

"No, just what's out there."

"Well, you want to do me a favor and go *look* in the back?"

"We don't even have a 'back.' We just have an 'out there.' If you haven't seen it out there, then there's no such thing. I'd go with what you already got there."

But still, we look. I've seen men—adult men, mature men, experienced men—sow their wild oats, find a wonderful mate, and say, "That's it, I'm ready to settle down." Then a woman from another country walks by— "Hey,

I didn't know *she* was out there. I may have spoken too soon. . . . Apparently *she* is a consideration as well. . . ."

Again, I refer you to my dog.

Did you ever ask a dog if they want to go out for a walk *while* they're already out for a walk? They still get excited. The fact that they're currently enjoying a walk doesn't matter. They want to see what a *different* walk would be like.

Sometimes I'm embarrassed by how powerful the "turn around and look" instinct is. I was once driving and saw a woman driving by in the opposite direction, and I actually turned around to look. I'm staring at her *car.* I'm basically straining to look at the rear end of a Toyota Camry, but still, I felt the need to look.

I'm not proud of this, you understand, I'm just saying.

Often, the curiosity we have is very limited, and very specific, and surprisingly *tame.* I know many is the occasion I've seen an attractive woman, and all I've wanted to say was, "Excuse me, but could I just feel your calf?"

More as a research project than anything else. "I was interested in the area on your back—just above your belt. It has an alluring muscularity, yet it's in no way unfeminine. What exactly would that feel like? Rather smooth and nice, I'd imagine. May I?"

And then, with her blessing, you feel the back, and you're done.

"Just as I imagined: Fleshy and Good. Taut, yet not unyielding. Thank you." And you go on your way.

I was recently out for dinner with my loved one and noticed a striking woman sitting a few tables over. Now, because I'm not an idiot, I made a point of not noticing her. You wouldn't believe how I didn't notice her. She could have burst into flames—I'm telling you, I wouldn't have noticed.

My wife notices I'm not noticing.

She says, "She *is* cute."

"Who?"

" 'Who?' " she says, mocking me. "Miss 110 pounds of blonde over there."

"Where?"

"Oh stop."

I didn't even get credit for not looking. I was apparently whimpering like a dog trying not to go for the biscuit on his nose.

Now, if you're ever out with the One For Whom You've Forsaken All Others, and you do find you're inadvertently gazing at an Other, you can try to recover some dignity by pretending you're looking for some specific reason.

"Hey, Honey, doesn't that woman look like your cousin Cheryl?"

And if they want to cooperate, they'll say, "Where? *Her?* She looks nothing like Cheryl." And you laugh it off. "I guess I'm just a big idiot," and you keep walking.

Or, you say, "Hey, look at that girl over there. She's got a stomach like a guy."

Your loved one turns around. "Where?"

"Oh, you can't see it now. She just sat down."

The key to this one is bringing it up *first*. Otherwise, you have that much more ill will to overcome.

Now again, I'm not *proud* of any of this behavior. I'm just passing it on to you, the consumer.

Sometimes, you can *both* stare at people and enjoy a rousing game of "Let's Figure Out What's Wrong with *Them*." Fun in airports, restaurants, wherever you go.

"See that girl over there—with the earrings? She's with security. Used to be CIA."

"Okay. The guy over there—eating by himself? Just broke up with his girlfriend."

"*No,* she left *him*."

"For her aerobics instructor."

"Good call."

"Okay, okay, okay—the lady over there, with the two kids? Those are not her children."

"She's not even related."

"She takes different children out every weekend, because she loves children but is sadly unable to have any of her own."

"Because of a radiation leak in the town where her husband used to work."

"Which killed him, by the way."

"Yeah, because otherwise, how come he's not here?"

"Exactly."

Watching other *couples* is even more fun. You can make up stories *and* be really judgmental at the same time.

"Oh, they're not happy at all."

"No, they're not. . . . Look how he doesn't look at her when she's talking."

"Just keeps eating his soup. . . . She's talking, he's eating. . . ."

"You know, they haven't made love in over five months."

"Because he's cheating on her."

"And she knows about it."

"Of course she knows."

"That's what she's talking about. She knows who the woman is, where they've been meeting. . . ."

"And he can't look up because she'll see it in his eyes—"

"And she'll know she's right."

"Of course she's right."

"Bastard."

"Makes me sick."

Of course, sometimes it backfires and blows up in your face.

"See that couple over there?"

"Yeah?"

"Look how he keeps squeezing her arm. And he really looks at her when she's talking. I love that."

"*I* look at you when you're talking. . . . I mean, not *now,* because we're looking at them, but ordinarily. . . ."

"Are they more affectionate than us?"

"No."

"They look really affectionate."

"They're not. They're exactly the same amount affectionate as we are. In fact, if anything, less so."

Then we watch them a little more desperately, looking for flaws.

"Do you like her hair?"

"Why?"

"Just tell me my hair doesn't look like that."

"It doesn't."

"Really?"

"You can't even compare. You have beautiful hair, and hers is all dyed and yucky and stupid. She has stupid hair."

"She really does, doesn't she?"

"I'm telling you."

A moment. "Then how come he's so affectionate?"

Bing-
Bang-
Boom

──────────────── Sexually speaking, when two people first get together, it's easy to be impressive. They've never seen the show before, so every trick is a crowd pleaser.

"Watch this. You watching? Hey—look at that. Didn't expect *that*, did you? Of course not. I'm very, very good."

But after a while, you run out of tricks. The bag is empty. The lights go up, and you have to tell the truth. "Ummm, that's basically it. That's all I know. Good night everybody. . . . Drive safely."

You can't even *think* of what else could be done. You

273

both just accept that this is pretty much what it's going to be for the rest of your lives.

Of course, the *big* fear would be that they're *not* impressed. "That doesn't feel good? Really. Hmm. In my last relationship, that was a big hit. For six years, that was a very popular move. But you're saying it's actually more of an *irritant*? Hmm. Interesting. . . . I'd like you to see the show again tomorrow. This was an off night."

You know what ruins sex for a lot of guys? The letters to *Penthouse* magazine. Have you ever read them? Me neither, but a friend of mine did and he told me . . .

What they have are letters written by presumably normal people like ourselves, and we read them and go, "Where does this happen? I've never heard anything like this. *I've* picked up hitchhikers, they didn't do any of that. They just got out of the car when we got there, and left."

And all these boasting figures: "I've never considered myself big, but at eleven inches . . ." Oh come on. My *leg* is eleven inches.

They don't realize I *want* these letters to be true. I'm rooting for them. And if it doesn't sound exactly true, I'll bend the truth. I'll work around it, give them the benefit of the doubt.

Because they start off normal enough: "I went down

to get the mail, but to my surprise, the regular mailman had been replaced by a beautiful blond woman. . . ."

Okay, that's not crazy. Why not? A blond person delivers his mail—maybe he lives in Milwaukee, heavy Scandinavian population . . .

". . . It was a hot day, she came inside, I offered her a drink, she took off her shirt . . ."

Okay, that's not crazy. It's hot, maybe she had that shirt-sticking-to-your-back-thing going on, so she *had* to take it off. . . . So far, he's not lying.

". . . We had a few drinks, suddenly one thing led to another, and we were all over each other. I was here, she was there . . . we were touching, we were rubbing, we were biting . . . Suddenly, my neighbor, a bikini model who was recently widowed, comes in and *she* gets in the action, too . . ."

Alright. Maybe the neighbor was concerned. She heard the furniture being tossed about, she was alarmed. She comes in, they're naked, she's dressed—she was embarrassed. No one likes to be overdressed. So she strips down and gets in there, too. So far, he's writing an honest letter.

". . . We're touching, we're moving, and these three cheerleaders were coming home from practice . . ."

Who's to say he *doesn't* live near a high school?

". . . Now the *six* of us are rolling around my Barca-Lounger . . ."

And then he goes too far.

". . . And after nine hours, we took a shower and did it again."

You did not! You did nothing of the kind. Why can't you just be honest? "After nine hours, I had a heart attack and almost died." Then, I could have sympathy for the guy. "Well, sure you got hurt, look what you tried to do. That's too much."

Just be honest. That's all.

T he big problem with sex, I believe, is faulty advertising. It's always sold as something "to be shared" by two people.

Right there: the word "share." That's where the problem starts.

Sex is not about sharing. It never was and it never will be.

I don't care how sensitive you think you are, if you're making love, and you freeze-frame the action, at any given second, *one* of the two people is thinking: "I hope this feels good for *you* because *I* got a cramp you wouldn't believe. . . . No kidding around, I have no feeling in my left hip. . . . That last little motion was entirely for *your* benefit."

You're either giving or you're taking.

"That was for *you,* this is for *me.* This is for you,

that's for me. . . ." You take turns. You alternate. The trick is to alternate quickly and consistently enough, so the whole thing is a big blur and everyone goes home a winner.

Even kissing is complicated.

Kissing is a wonderful thing, but there's an inherent design flaw: I don't think anyone's face is supposed to be that close to your face for that length of time.

It's just odd. If for no other reason, it's frightening. Why do you think people close their eyes when they kiss? Think about it. In the real world, if you saw someone an inch and a half away, coming at you with their eyes open and their lips puckered, you'd scream. It's alarming.

Plus, it's not particularly flattering. For either of you. So you close your eyes. It's safe; no one has to know what you look like in that condition.

We close our eyes *unless* the kiss goes on a really long time. If the kiss goes on too long, you will *sneak open* one eye and *peek* at the other person.

Everyone does this, and I'm not sure why. I guess we want to make sure it's still going on. Because that would make you look dumb—the kiss is over and no one told you. You're still going and she's reading a magazine— you're going to look very bad.

Sometimes people open their eyes just to *check* on the other person. This happens in new relationships. There are too many unknowns. So if you're kissing, and she momentarily takes her hand off your back, you get nervous. "Where's her hand going? What is she—going to stab me?" You open that eye right up.

Maybe she's using the free hand to steal things. "I could've sworn I had an ashtray right there. . . . This lunatic is swiping ashtrays from right under my nose."

So you sneak a peek. Just to be sure. Which is only fair, because while you were still kissing, she was sneaking peeks at *you.*

A very unfortunate moment is when you both sneak a peek at the same time. This is not good. Because now what you have is two human heads with their lips locked and their eyes wide open. There's no romance, there's no passion—there's nothing. There's just someone standing very close with their nose against *your* nose. The whole concept of kissing becomes suddenly grotesque and perverse.

And you both get defensive.

"What are you looking at?"

"What are *you* looking at?"

"I wasn't looking."

"I *saw* you looking."

"Yeah, well, you wouldn't have noticed *me* looking if *you* weren't looking in the first place."

"Look, this is obviously not working. Why don't we just call it a night, huh? Just put the ashtray back and we'll forget the whole thing ever happened."

Sometimes, even with a partner you know by heart, you can be jolted with new information.

One night, after what I thought was a particularly impressive display of sexual know-how, I turned to my bride, very proud of myself, and with a knowing smile said, "Not too shabby, huh?"

I actually said that.

(I share this with you, and no one else.)

She smiles back, but not enough. I know something's wrong.

"What?"

She says, gently, "I didn't really have the moment I think you think I had."

I'm confused. "What are you talking about? *Sure* you did."

"No, I didn't."

"Yes you did."

"Okay, when? When did I have that moment?"

"Before. When you made that sound. Don't you remember? Right before I made that sound that *I* made."

"I remember *that*."

"Yeah well, I never would have made that sound if you hadn't made your little throaty noise first. I took my cue from *you*."

She says, "I didn't give any cue."

"Well, correct me if I'm wrong, but when you make that sound . . ."—and I demonstrated; people really hate when you do that—"when you make that sound, is that not like a signal for 'Hello, we have a winner'?"

She pauses. "Sometimes."

My brain races. "What do you mean 'sometimes'?"

"I mean *sometimes* it means that and sometimes it means I'm just very close."

Now, understand: This is not someone I just met. This is a woman I've known for many years. And this is something I honestly never heard.

"You're kidding me, right?"

"No."

"There's no way you could expect me to know that."

She says, "Well, *now* you know."

"Yeah, but it's a little late now. You can't make the same sound to mean two different things."

"I can't?"

I was adamant. "No, you can't. You have to have two distinct sounds. One for 'Thank you, no more calls' and another one for 'We still need a few more calls to hit our goal.' "

She looks at me, sees that sadly I'm not joking. "Fine. I will try to distinguish my sounds."

"Please. That's all I'm asking. Let's lock this down. Because, hey, this is for *your* benefit—not mine."

See, I don't think women understand this. The whole concept of the sensitive, giving, patient lover is not something that comes to men instinctively.

Obviously. We're the ones who made up the Bing-Bang-Boom approach. And not because we're bad people —it is simply that *that's* how we would make love if we were by ourselves.

And I'll tell you something else: Even within the Bing-Bang-Boom, we only made up the "Bing" and the "Bang" to get the "Boom." "Boom" was the objective the whole time.

But we came up with the "Bing" and the "Bang." Why? Because we care. We're out there, making an effort.

I'm simply saying, we're potentially even worse than you think, so please, give us a little credit here.

Pain,

Humiliation,

and

the Great

Outdoors

One of the reasons people get married is suntan lotion; you're going to need help. There are parts of your back that you simply can't get to by yourself, and quite frankly, no one is going to do it for you who *isn't* married to you.

My fear of getting burned goes back to being a kid, when you not only had the pain but the humiliation bonus the next day when you had to wear a T-shirt in the water. Nothing more embarrassing than that one. Just a big advertisement to the community that you have no common sense whatsoever. "*You* all put on lotion and didn't get burned; I myself was careless and stupid, and I now wear this Garment of Shame before the entire bathing population."

And you get the little air bubble under the T-shirt, which provided your friends something extra to pull, thereby adding another layer of pain on top of the humiliation. All in all, a pleasant outing.

Nowadays, people flee the sun. With all the technological and medical discoveries, we've been reduced to cavemen again. "Ugh, Big Round Thing in Sky— *BAD.*"

And there are so many choices in Suntanning maintenance. They're numbered 1 to 125. Who knows *that specifically* how they want to be tanned? And unless you know your exact latitude, longitude, and the speed of the Earth's orbit, you're just winging it anyway. "Let me see, it's very hot out, the winds are coming from the east, I'm originally from the Northwest . . . I'm going to go with Number 15. Yeah, 15 sounds good for me."

You just want to be better protected than the guy lying next to you. "What does he have—a 20? I'm going to get a 25."

It becomes a competition.

"Oh yeah? I see your 25 and raise you a plastic nose guard and a PABA hat."

We once went to a nude beach, the logic being: It's 140 degrees, why not scorch *everything*?

The thing about being naked in public is—there's nothing you can think about except how naked you are. And how naked everybody else is. That's all you see.

You don't think, "There's a tall guy." It's, "There's a *naked* guy." You don't say, "That woman looks like a lovely person." You say, "There's a *naked* lady."

And you think about your clothes. When you're dressed, you never think about your clothes. You never walk down the street conscious of your clothes, thinking, "I love my pants. I'm happy to have my pants." But when you're naked, you can't get past, "I have no pants. I'm walking, and I'm very much without trousers." That's all you think about: the absence of places to put your hands.

You know how when you're in the water, you have very little body weight? This is another gift that nature provides to help keep men and women together. Men love it because with one hand you can lift the entire person you're married to. And this works out for both of you, because in one shot, you feel strong and she feels thin. While she's thinking, "I really *am* losing weight," you're busy thinking, "I am the Strongest Man in the World."

You have to appreciate these Little Things in life, because the Big Things may never get here, and then you've hung around for nothing.

My personal favorite is when you go swimming, and two hours later, hot water leaks out of your ear. For no reason. Out of nowhere, you just get this little, warm release in your ear, and all of a sudden, you're hearing better. You didn't even know you were hearing badly. It's just a bonus from God. You're thinking, "Gee, I'm not complaining, it's good, everything's good," and then all of a sudden, "Even better." You gotta love that.

Being near water is supposed to be "calming"; apparently, you can "breathe" your problems out across the ocean.

I keep trying this, but in the middle of breathing out, I always think, "Someone's going to be breathing this *in*. These problems have to end up *somewhere*." I envision some poor guy on the coast of Japan, trying to relax, and suddenly he's got my problems. He doesn't need that. He's walking around going, "Gee, I got to send a note to Aunt Essie, thank her for the sweater—I don't even know who she is."

And my next thought is, "Forget about that—what about *his* problems? I don't want them washing back to *me*." We could each potentially be walking around with problems neither of us are prepared to handle. Suddenly this whole "breathing and relaxing" thing is not as simple as it's cracked up to be.

It's not easy to ever truly "get away from it all," because like they say, "Wherever you go, there you are." (Again, I couldn't tell you who They are, but trust me—they said it.)

I mean, I love going for walks in the mountains, but I always feel I kind of look wrong. Like people can tell I'm faking it. I've been hiking happily and had people stop me, presuming my car broke down.

I'm not sure what the actual difference is between "hiking" and just "walking." Is it speed? Intent? It may be related to the type of pants you're wearing. Shorts that come close to the knees can turn "walking" into "hiking" like *that*.

Also to be considered is What You Look At. If you're just going from Point A to Point B, it's "walking," but if you stop and point at a tree, it's "hiking." Even a simple "Oh, look—a bird" automatically makes you a "hiker." So, if that's not what you had in mind, for God's sake be careful what you point at.

Our friends have this cabin on a lake, and they invited us up to go fishing.

Now, having grown up in the city, I wasn't a big "fishing" guy. Didn't fish on any regular basis. You *can* fish in the city, but you catch things you're not that happy to have—like a snow tire and a union organizer. Nothing that you would actually heat up with a touch of lemon and serve to company.

So we're fishing and my wife had a problem with killing the fish.

I wasn't crazy with that part either, but I figured, "If we just wait for them to die naturally, it could take forever. Certainly till after supper."

Most people like to distance themselves from the dirty work. Like a Mob hit. "Look, do what you gotta do. I don't want to know, I don't want to be involved. . . . I'll eat the thing, I just don't want my name coming up, understand?"

To me, killing fish is not as cruel as the fact that we *tease* them first. We dangle worms and things they like, so they think they're getting a snack, when in fact what they're getting is death. It's not honest.

We advertise worms, then go, "You know what? We're all out of worms. How would you like a big hook in your mouth instead?" The ultimate Bait and Switch.

And fish, God bless them, are so dumb, they simply do not catch on. How many years have we been fishing? A zillion years? They haven't figured it out? All it would take is one fish to see the worm and say, "Wait a second. . . .

Worms don't just dangle like that. . . . Something's going on here. . . . HEY!"

But they don't. They line up. They see their friends getting yanked out of the water, and they don't care. They're cocky. "Don't worry, Honey, that won't happen to me. He didn't know what he was doing, whereas— OWWWWW! . . . This one's got a hook, too!"

They don't see that whole pattern. Worm / death. Worm / death. *I* would catch on. If I went to a restaurant, and every time I ordered fruit cup, somebody dropped an anvil on my head, I would begin to notice. "Hmm. . . . Fruit cup / death. Fruit cup / death. You know what? I'm gonna get the soup instead."

Fish—they're in schools, but they're just not learning.

I tried to convince my wife that fish don't *feel* the hook.

She says, "How do *you* know?"

I said, "I *don't,* but that's what they say."

She had no argument. "Well, okay then, if you're sure that's what they say. . . ."

Again, why would They lie?

But I'm sure animals say the same things about *us.* Go into the woods and you'll hear grizzly bears saying, "You know when you bite people's arms off? They don't feel it. Believe me, if I thought they felt it, I could never do it. I wouldn't be able to live with myself. No, you know why they're screaming and jumping around like that? It's a dance. It's the Dance of Joy. They're saying, 'Yippee! Thanks for trimming that section off me.' Every six months, they shed that part of their bodies naturally. . . . That's why they have those short-sleeve shirts. It's part of nature—don't worry about it."

Apparently we only get upset about killing animals if they're cute. Like dolphins. We get all upset when dolphins get caught in tuna nets, but no one cares about the 10,000 dead tuna on the same boat. Little ugly tunas, one on top of the other, screaming for help, "Hey, someone get this crate off my eye!" No one's concerned.

Because they're not *cute*. Dolphins, on the other hand, have that great round, smiling face, the friendly eyes, the bald head—they look like your Uncle Marvin. We can't slaughter anything that looks like it might show up for the Holidays.

We're outraged when other cultures eat animals we don't. "They eat *dogs*? That's disgusting. They're savages. How could someone eat a dog?!"

But chickens? Who cares? "Cut it up, put it in a bucket, we'll eat it in the car."

They're not cute. "Boy, look at that chicken! With

the triangle-on-the-head thing—it's *so* ugly! But you better put that puppy down, buddy!"

Puppies are adorable. But lobsters? "Boil that one alive—it'll teach him a lesson. . . . Fix yourself up, like the Labradors. . . . Make an *effort*!"

It's like fur. We hate the idea of killing baby seals and foxes and minks—but there'd be no problem if someone showed up in a nice full-length Rat Coat. Or a double-breasted Weasel Jacket. Nobody would care. It's the same way we treat each other: penalize the unattractive, idolize the cute.

M y favorite time of year to be outdoors is the Fall. I love that whole Autumn, New England, wear-a-big-sweater-have-hot-chocolate-listen-to-depressing-music-cry-in-your-dorm-with-Ali-MacGraw-*Love-Story* kind of thing. That image was such a part of growing up that I was genuinely surprised to get to college and find Ali MacGraw not already there and crying about something I said. I thought that just came automatically.

But even *without* Ms. MacGraw, I've always found Fall to be an achingly romantic time of year. As it turns out, it's not the location or the weather—it's Tweed. There's something about tweed that makes you fall in love. I'm telling you—you put on a tweed jacket or an itchy sweater, and in half an hour, you're going to meet someone and get involved. Maybe it's the itching of the tweed. It could be that as you're standing there talking, you find yourselves scratching and pulling till one of you says, "Look, why don't we go somewhere and get out of these clothes." And in less than half an hour, you're in a dorm, scantily clad and chatting.

And of course, if you add *crunching leaves* to that, you can knock it down to fifteen, twenty minutes. Crunching leaves is very romantic. "Crunching" and "itching" *together* is almost overpowering. I'm telling you—hot cocoa, a couple of leaves, and tweed—you're all set. Sometimes even a tight undershirt and a bowl of potato chips will do the trick—as long as you're itching and crunching.

Last Fall, we took a trip back East and drove through some beautiful farm country. Now, as you may know, there happens to be a particular, distinctive aroma around farms, and no matter how many times you've experienced it, no matter how old you are or how smart you are, you automatically turn to the other person in the car and casually ask, "Is that you?"

Now, you *know* it's not, but you always ask.

"Is that you?"

There are very few dumber questions. Because, essentially, what you're asking is, "Is that *you,* or 7,000 acres of manure? Which of the two am I contending with here? Is it miles and miles of punishingly nasty steer funk, or just something that happened to you for a second? I can't distinguish."

I got news for you: If there's truly a chance of confusing those two things, get out of the car and live by yourself.

Wish

You Were

Here

　　　　　　　　　　　　I'll tell you what I love about hotels: They can't do enough for you. They want to make you feel at home, and then they give you things that nobody has at home. Shower caps, shoe horns . . . and sewing kits? I have never sewn in my life. What makes them think I'm going to start in a Marriott in Cleveland? Has anybody ever made that call? "Honey, I'm in Ohio, and my buttons are flying off like crazy. There's a sewing kit right here. I have it. Talk me through."

　　And I love the little chocolates on the pillow. *There's* a clever snacking item, because personally, there's nothing I like better right before I go to bed than a nice diabetic seizure. A pound and a half of sugar before going to sleep, good idea.

I want to know how they selected chocolate as the appropriate treat. What were the other suggestions? "How about . . . scallops? Do you think scallops would be good on a pillow? Or maybe kiwi. Several kiwi, thinly sliced . . ."

When you're in a hotel without your partner, it's amazing what you'll do to entertain yourself. If you're there long enough, you will actually read the brochure with prices for carriage rides through the Old City. You pick up the phone book to see how many people with your last name live in town. When I was in Dallas, I actually looked to see if there were any Oswalds still living in the area; call them up and settle this thing once and for all.

And you watch TV you would never watch in real life. Those Specially-Selected-After-Hour-Movies? I love the editing decisions these guys make. They're the sleaziest movies in the world—cheesy looking, overlit, with bad music, pathetic acting, no story, and nothing in them *but* sex—but they still use "discretion" and never let you see *exactly* what's going on. They leave that final moment to the imagination, like, perhaps, at the last minute, her lips actually went around a cup of coffee she found in bed.

Of course the last indignity about these movies is that they show up on your bill.

"Okay, sir, that's three long-distance calls, a turkey club sandwich, a Diet Coke, and 'Melissa Goes to College' —apparently three times. . . . What a thirst for knowledge *she* must have."

But even regular TV—it's amazing what you'll watch.

Like the Discovery Channel.

When you have no place to go, you can't believe how long you'll watch this. An hour and a half watching a zebra chew a leaf.

I always feel bad for the TV networks, spending all this money on prime-time shows, big budget mini-series, and special events, when I'm in a Ramada Inn with a chef salad on my lap watching a badger eat a straw hat from nine to eleven.

And I love those talk shows. If you turn on Oprah, or Donahue, or Sally Jesse Raphael, and you see a panel of five women and one guy—you know the guy's in trouble.

You don't even have to hear what they're saying. You see the guy and you just know he's gonna have a very tough show. He either did something to these women, or he *failed* to do something for these women—whatever it is, he's just wrong.

I know it, you know it, yet these guys have no idea. If they did they wouldn't be on the show.

But they are literally without a clue. Their logic is, "I'm right, she's wrong, and if I go on national TV, everyone will take *my* side, and that'll be the end of that."

Then they share their story, and the guy just gets buried: "He doesn't come home for three days, and when he does, he brings his girlfriend to sleep with us."

The crowd boos and hisses.

The guy just smiles and looks to the audience for sympathy. "C'mon, she *knows* I love her."

Why do they go through this? So that the hostility they breed in their home can now be enjoyed on a national level?

And what about the car ride home? After the show. What could that be like? They've just slugged it out and spewed their mutual venom in front of millions of people, and they get into their car, look at each other, and say, "You wanna get something to eat?"

I just don't get it.

Eating on the road can be tough. You always feel so pathetic, sitting in a restaurant by yourself. "Look at that guy. He has no friends."

You try to look busy. You bring a newspaper, and you read it extremely thoroughly. Things you don't even care about—"Ooh look, the weather in Utah is apparently unseasonal." You just keep reading, as if to say, "I *have* friends, but with all this reading I have to do . . ."

And the people who work at the restaurant make it worse. Most tables are already set for two, and when they see you're by yourself, they immediately take away the *other* plate, to highlight for everybody else your lack of companion. "*He* will be alone. Furthermore, there's no chance of anyone joining him, because we've removed the plates and silverware." They also figure you're so depressed, you don't need that extra knife around.

The worst part of eating alone is that there's nobody there to tell you that you have food on your face—another reason people get married; someone to say, "Honey, right over there you got a little thing . . . nope . . . nope—got it."

You could actually finish an entire meal by yourself and leave the restaurant with food *still* on your face. Conceivably, you could walk into another restaurant later that day with food *already on your face.* That's the lowest thing there is. At least then, people will look at you and realize, "Well, that's why he's eating by himself. Look at him, he's got sandwich on his face."

I'll tell you something about traveling by yourself: It's ultimately very healthy for your relationship.

When you first learn that one of you has to go away, you're actually both looking forward to it, but neither of you wants to admit it. So you both pretend you're going to be miserable.

"I'm going to miss you."

"I'm *really* going to miss you."

Again, it's a competition.

"I'm the one unable to live without you."

"No, *I'm* totally unable to live without *you,* I swear."

The truth is, one of you is thrilled to be going somewhere, and the other one can't wait to have the house to themselves. Then, you get to where you're going, and you find you really *do* miss each other. If for no other reason, you forgot how to be alone.

"Honey, where are my keys? . . . Honey? . . . Oh, right, you're in Phoenix. . . . I'll just . . . find them myself. That's what I used to do, sure."

Sometimes you get homesick because where you went isn't all it was cracked up to be.

"You wouldn't believe the cheesy hotel they stuck me in. I wish you were here."

"To see the cheesy hotel?"

"Yes."

Or you just need to hear a sane voice. Ever call from a family get-together that *she* weaseled out of?

"Hi—I'm going to go OUT OF MY MIND."

"It's only for two more days."

"I won't make it, you hear me? I WON'T."

Then you start pining for home, like a child.

"How's the house?"

"What do you mean, 'How's the house?' "

"What does everything look like?"

"Since you left at four-thirty?"

"Yeah."

"It's all different. I repainted, knocked down the bathroom wall, and the garage is gone. No one knows what happened."

"How's the dog?"

"Fine."

"Does the dog miss me?"

"Been crying since you left."

"Seriously?"

"Seriously? The dog has no idea you're gone. Thinks you're in the shower. . . Would you like to know how *I* am?"

"Yes, yes, I was just going to ask. I swear—that was my next question. How are *you*?"

Those miles between you can really change things. You forget how to talk.

"What are you doing?"

"Nothing. Why?"

"You sound distracted."

"I'm not distracted."

"You watching TV?"

"No."

"So who's that talking?"

"You can *hear* that?"

"Yes, I can hear that. What are you watching, 'The Jeffersons'?"

"I'm not watching—it's just on."

"You're watching 'The Jeffersons' while you're talking to me?"

"I'm not watching it. I'll shut it off. Wait. . . . Okay, there you see, I shut it off. No more 'Jeffersons.'"

Then you're quiet. Then you tell her which episode of "The Jeffersons" you were watching. She saw that one. Actually liked it. You talk about Sherman Hemsley. Then you talk about what you used to watch when you came home from school as a kid. What you used to eat *while* you watched TV as a kid. You compare the merits of different snacking foods. Then one of you has the presence of mind to pull the plug.

"What are we doing here? We're talking long distance about Pepperidge Farm cookies."

You both say, "Good night."

You both say, "I love you."

You both point out how the other one sounds phony.

You sit and say nothing for a while.

You both promise to be better at this tomorrow and swear to never go away again.

Then you hang up, and one hour later you wake her up to find out how "The Jeffersons" ended.

Dear

Japan,

Stop!!!

————————At some point, my wife and I got ourselves on every mailing list in the free world. All you have to do is buy *one* distinctly dumb product you don't need, and everyone with a catalogue hears about it. "Hi! We understand you don't care *what* you spend money on anymore. We have just the catalogue for you."

I like the Combination Products. Things that you probably already have, but not in this particular combination.

"It's a sweater vest *and* a bottle opener."

"It's a hot beverage thermos *and* a snorkeling mask!"

And, of course, if you look at the pictures long

enough, you start thinking, "Well, you know, we *could* use that. With a thermos / snorkel mask, we wouldn't have to come up for coffee anymore. We could snorkel all day and never come up!"

Then they combine things that not only *shouldn't* be together, there's no way they *could* be. "It's a cassette rack *and* a Doberman pinscher!"

How could that be?

"It's a rain bonnet, but it's also your parents."

How could that be?! I just saw my parents. They weren't a rain bonnet.

They're doing it with stores now, too. Stores are branching out into areas where they have no business doing business. "Beauty Supplies and Cheese," "Massage Tables and Skate Repairs."

There's a cabinet store in my neighborhood that sells bookcases, shelves, and pineapple juice. Apparently, that was where they felt they were lacking—the juice market.

"Look, we already have a hammer and a flat surface; go get a pineapple, we'll make juice."

Even the fast-food places—everybody's trying to do everyone else's job. Hamburger places have pizza, pizza places have salad bars, chicken places have croissants, bakeries are developing film—everybody's so desperate:

"Don't go anywhere else. We'll get you whatever you want —just stay here!"

But the catalogues are dangerous because they seduce you with the pictures you can peruse at your leisure.

Victoria's Secret is big trouble. That's a good-looking catalogue. That one I don't throw out so fast.

In all fairness, it's *more* than a catalogue. It's a lovely story, a novella, really, that I keep by my bedside, and every night I read a few pages and see what those wacky girls are up to this time.

There are no *words,* of course, but you can put together the story. It's about a group of women, a Slumber Party Organization. I don't know what their particular agenda is; I don't know if it's a political assembly or more a social, community-minded, grass-roots type of thing. But I *do* know they get together every couple of months to, apparently, slumber.

They meet at this great hunting lodge one of them owns, and though they're obviously very close, there's tremendous anxiety regarding their attire. They're just not sure what to wear. And this is where the drama comes in. The conflict.

They each bring a couple of changes, and they try them on for each other, hoping to gain the approval of this very rigid group. They slip into something— "What do you think? No? Okay, I'll try on something else." And then someone else takes the floor. Many of them are quite distraught and end up standing on the porch alone, so demanding are the slumbering wardrobe requirements.

One woman wearing a peach negligee comes in and leans on the piano.

"Better! That's definitely a piano type of garment. Make sure there's a baby grand around when you wear that, because it really accents the weave."

Trying on, taking off. Trying on, taking off. On and off it goes. Until finally, content with their choices, they proceed to slumber.

A couple of pages of women sleeping, and then, toward the end of the book, you notice they're modeling the heavier stuff: sweaters, coats, luggage, and gloves. That's because they're leaving.

It's the end of the party, and they're getting ready to go home. But though the chapter is ending, you *know* they're coming back next month, because they never tell you which one is Victoria, and what's the big secret.

There are catalogues that my wife gets excited about that absolutely fly under my radar. I never even know about them till things show up in the mail.

"Where'd we get this?"

"I ordered it," says the woman I love.

"What is it?"

"Tea cozy."

"A what?"

"A *tea* cozy."

I run those two words around in my head for a few seconds, thinking that will help me.

"Okay, I don't know what that is."

"It's a thing, you put it over a pot of tea, and it keeps it—"

"Cozy?"

"Exactly."

"Good. Because that's the one thing I felt our tea was lacking: that certain coziness."

When a catalogue comes to our house, we're both free to browse through it. But with other types of mail, territories need to be defined.

Whose mail is whose? If it's addressed to both of you, who gets to open it first? If it's addressed to *one* of you, but you know that it's going to be for both of you anyway, are you allowed to read it without your spouse pursuing felony charges?

And what about letters that truly *are* personal? Friends that you knew before you were a couple and never bothered to talk about? Old lovers? The very delivery of one of these letters can drive a wedge right through your home.

"Who is that?"

"I told you about her."

"Never."

"No?"

"Trust me."

"Well, probably because I haven't spoken to her in fifteen years."

"Why would she write to you now?"

"I don't know."

"Does she know you're married?"

"I'm not sure."

"What does she want?"

"I don't know—*you* have the letter, you tell *me*."

"I *had* the letter—I threw it out."

I think it's amazing that any mail is ever delivered in this country.

Have you ever dropped a letter into one of those mailboxes on the side of the road, isolated, in the middle of nowhere? I always think, "They don't know this mailbox is here. I might as well be throwing it in the garbage." How do they remember where all the mailboxes are? Do they update the list? I don't think they do.

But we have faith.

We trust that they will deliver our mail—anywhere we want. And for only 29 cents. Isn't that remarkable? We tell them, "Take this piece of paper to Bangor, Maine, and for your efforts, I will give you a quarter and four pennies."

And they do it. Would *you* do it? No. But they're wonderful people. Devoted men and women, forming a human chain of hands, taking my little letter across the country.

You can't scare them. "My friend lives in North Dakota, on a hill, it's really pretty remote, the door is in the back . . ." And they go, "Don't worry, we'll find him. Is this his name—'Ed'? Just give us three days, and 29 cents . . . that's all we ask."

Even *they* know that 29 cents is a bargain. And a lot of times they kind of—lose it. That's why, if you give them real money—10 bucks—they guarantee it. "For 10 bucks, there's no fooling around. For 29 cents, there *is* some fooling around, we'll grant you that."

It's like greasing a guy in Vegas. "Tell you what, for 10 bucks, I'll take care of you. I'll bring this to Ed. For 15 bucks, I'll bring you back a little piece of paper that tells you Ed got it. For 40 bucks, I'll bring back *Ed.*"

Whether it's stuff in a catalogue or stuff in a store, my problem is I have zero sales resistance. I am a salesman's dream. All they have to do is tell me one reason why I'd be stupid *not* to buy something, and I buy it. Because I don't want them to think I'm stupid.

I was in this stereo store, looking at this VCR / CD

player / laser disc / pants presser combination thing. I wasn't even thinking of getting it, I was just playing.

Salesman comes over. "You know, that CD player'll hold up to 20 discs at a time."

"Yeah?"

He says, "Yes-siree-bob. That's at least 18 hours of music."

"Okey-dokey." And he wraps it up.

You see, he opened my eyes. I hadn't done the arithmetic. Eighteen hours, sure. Who wouldn't want *that*?

Then I got it home and realized, "Wait a second! I'm not *up* 18 hours. When would I use this? The last four hours will actually be keeping me awake. This is not something I need."

I'd have to get up at four in the morning just to program this thing. "Honey, wake up. Any thoughts about what you might want to hear tonight at two in the morning? I've got Springsteen, I've got Mozart, Gerry and the Pacemakers—everything. I have a Vaughn Meader record in there. Help me, I have nothing left."

You know why I got this thing, truthfully? Because I wanted one more remote control unit in my life. Can never have too many remote controls, I say. I now have twelve of them lined up on the table. I invite friends over and say, "See those? They're all mine. And I don't know how to work *any* of them. Not *one* button do I understand, but I know they're mine."

I own things that I myself can't operate. It's embarrassing. Friends say, "Hey, did you tape that show?" and I'll have to tell them "I tried, but something happened. I just got fuzz and the sound to a Jimmy Durante movie. And by the way, did you call this month? My answering machine is flashing that somebody called, but it won't tell me who. Was it you? I'm asking everybody."

The problem is, they keep coming up with technology nobody asks for. They believe we *want* Freeze Frame Search, and Split Screen, and 14-Day Timers. Clocks that make coffee and cameras that talk. We don't want that. You know what I want? I just want to lie down. That's really all I want. If I could lie down for half an hour, I'd be so happy. I've been reading instructions since 1987, my head is pounding, I can't do it.

I want to write a letter:

"Dear Japan, STOP!!! We're fine. This is plenty of stuff. Why don't you stop with the VCRs and work on diseases. Go cure a disease—I'm going to figure out my cordless phone."

I think the reason we have trouble mastering our new toys is that there's simply no more room in our brains. At a certain point in life, your brain just says, "Thank you, but we're closed. Packed solid. We're not accepting any new information."

I am an adult man, and I am genuinely unable to learn anything new. Even simple stuff. Phone numbers.

If I have to call up Information for a number, I can't take all seven digits. It's too much. I have to split it with whoever is in the room.

Operator says, "That's three-eight-four . . ."

I throw it to my wife. "Three-eight-four—that's yours, you got it?"

". . . six-five-two-four."

"Okay, six-five-two-four."

Hang up. Plant it in your head. "Six-five-two-four. Six-five-two-four . . ."

"Okay, what was the first part?"

She looks up. "I forgot."

"You *forgot*? How could you forget? I had FOUR numbers and I still have them." You have to redial. "I'm sorry to bother you for that number again, but my wife got distracted and failed the small task given her. Could we have another chance, please?"

Sometimes I can remember a number if there's a pattern. Like a couple of pairs. "Three-eight-two, five-five, eight-eight." At least they're trying to work with you.

Sometimes you get a straight flush and you're thrilled.

"Give me a call when you get a chance. My new number is two-three-four, five-six-seven-eight."

"What are you—kidding me? I'll call you every day. That's just a gorgeous, gorgeous number. I'm going to call you five or six times a day. In fact, hang up right now. I wanna call you again, just to use it."

When you move, they give you a new number, and you don't have much say in what you get. And you should, because it's a big thing. A phone number is like your name; you want to get a good one.

A bad number is embarrassing. "Aw, look what they gave us—seven digits, no sequence, no pattern, no repeats —this is *CRAP*. No one's going to call us. Would you call a number like that? *I* wouldn't. Ahhh . . . Why even *have* a phone with a number like that? I'd rather move again and take our chances."

Sometimes you get desperate to make your number memorable.

If there's no pattern in the numbers, look for one on the keypad.

"Ooh—it's a little square. . . . It's a 'Z,' a little Zorro with a hat. It's a little couch and an ottoman—that's what it is: ottoman, couch, hat—call me."

Or you change the numbers to *letters,* hoping it spells something cute. "SNOOPY-5." "Yippy-I-O-Ki-eight." Problem is, your friends are too embarrassed to use it. They're adults, telling the operator, "Yes, that's a collect call to 'INKY-DINKY-DOO.' . . . I don't know the actual numbers, ma'am, all I know is Inky-Dinky-Doo. Let's not belabor this.''

For years they've been promising us phones where you can *see* who you're talking to. I think they're putting it off because if people could see you, you wouldn't be able to *lie* anymore. You can't say, "Oh, I was just leaving." They *see* you're in your pajamas, they *know* you're not leaving.

That's why we have answering machines—so they can lie for us. "We're not in right now . . ." Of course we're in.

"We can't get to the phone right now . . ." We could get to the phone if we wanted to. We just don't feel like it.

And friends get so upset when they find out you're "screening" your calls—listening to see who it is before you pick up. What are they upset about? They don't know you're screening till you pick it up, and if you do pick it up, it means they passed the audition. They're in. But they get so insecure. Even when you *are* out, they're convinced you're actually there and snubbing them. And they leave you those lengthy, pathetic messages.

"Are you there? . . . I know you're there. . . . I'll wait. . . . I'll wait all day. . . . Come on, you're not there? Really? Last chance . . . Okay, I just wanted to let you know that our machine is busted, so if you call and we

don't answer, it's because we're not here. . . . Hello?
. . . Oh, I thought I heard you pick up. . . ."

And I like when *older* people call our house. They
still don't quite get the concept of answering machines,
and talk to it like it's a secretary. "Yeah, um, please tell
Paul to call me. . . . I'm his aunt."

Deciding who gets to record the outgoing message on
your answering machine is a big deal. It's very important,
because *that* person represents the house. One of you gets
singled out to maitre d' the calls.

And it affects the callers. If my voice is on the tape,
my friends just start talking to me.

"Hey, it's me. You were right—that girl you were
telling me about really is cute. Call me."

Implication: "I don't even know you got married."

If my wife's voice is on the tape, they'll go, "Hey you
guys, how you doing? Good? Good. Paul, call me."

Implication: "I greet you both, but I'm interested in
only one."

You may suggest leaving a joint message. Can't. It's
too cutesy and no one will like you.

See, answering machines are hard appliances to
share. I know when I check the messages, I treat them
differently if they're not for me. I'll jot it down, but there's
not a lot of attention to details.

I'll say, "Debbie called."

"Debbie who?"

"Debbie."

"No last name?"

"I figured you'd know."

"I don't know any 'Debbie.' "

"How about Bebbie? Webbie?"

"What did she say?"

"Call her."

"Did she leave a number?"

"She said you have it."

"Under what?"

"Bebbie Webbie?"

Is This Kid Beautiful, or What?

At this point in our lives, everyone we know or ever heard of has a baby. I'm telling you, babies are unbelievably popular. Bigger than the Hula Hoop.

And for people who have babies, it's not enough that *they* have babies: They want *you* to have a baby.

"When are you going to have a baby? You two should really have a baby."

They have this plan for Nonstop Life Momentum, and they insist you play. When you're single, they nag you: "When are you going to get married?" When you get married, it's: "When are you going to have a kid?" You have a kid: "You should have a *second* kid—for the sake of

327

the *first* kid." It's always something. I'm sure when I'm eighty, they'll be asking, "So . . . when are you going to die?"

What is the rush with everybody? What do they—need my spot?

I think they just want the company. In case they don't enjoy it, they won't be the only ones who made a huge blunder with their lives. This way, they can drag you down *with* them. "You should really have a kid, you don't know what you're missing."

Sure I do. What am I—blind? I see what goes on, and it's not entirely appealing.

One time, we were on a plane, and this woman came on board with the Youngest Baby in the United States. Eleven minutes old. My guess is he was born *at* the baggage check-in counter; that's the only way he could have made the flight.

She sat in front of us and put the kid up on her shoulder, so he was hanging over the back of the seat, facing me. His little knuckles gripped the headrest, his tiny chin in the middle—like a miniature Kilroy Was Here.

Now, at one point we hit some turbulence. The guy sitting next to me slept right through it, but *I* was a little queasy, and then I looked up and noticed the baby had actually started changing colors. He went from yellow to green, to blue, a little paisley pattern, and then back to green. I thought to myself, "Okay, here we go, show time!" and I scooted over toward my wife.

Then I did something I'm not that proud of: I reached up and turned the kid's head to face the sleeping guy. Just angled it away from me a little. I figured, he'll never know—he's sleeping. So, after a few minutes of shaking around, the kid, who was now some deep shade of *mauve,* made a little coughing noise, and then, a thing came out of his mouth, that to this day I don't know what it was. It was like a grape, but different. Food that had no origin in our culture. It shot out and hit the guy's head.

The guy must have had kids of his own, because he just cleaned up his head and went back to sleep.

I, on the other hand—if that ever happened to *me,* I would have to insist that you kill me. Just put a bullet in the side of my head and end the whole thing.

I mean, if it were your own baby, that's one thing; you'd accept it. But someone else's baby? A strange baby? How do you just go back to your life? And it's not that I wouldn't want to go on living, I just wouldn't know how. How do you assimilate that event in with everything else you have planned? Your friend picks you up at the airport and asks, "How was your flight?" What do you say? "Well, a baby cheesed on my head, but otherwise, fine."

You're just going to carry on with your afternoon? I think not.

Babies have to put up with some pretty disgusting practices themselves.

I saw a kid who had some little dried-up food on his face. (Not since birth, just since lunch, I imagine.) His mother took out a tissue, *spit* on the tissue, and rubbed it into the kid's face. I'm not making this up. This goes on, in communities around our country, on a daily basis. It's enough to break your heart. You know that if babies could talk, that'd be the first thing they'd bring up. "Hey, don't do that. It's revolting. Would you like it if someone did that to you? Okay, then."

It is disgusting, but it sure does work, doesn't it? There's something in Mother Saliva that cleans like nobody's business. All women, once they give birth, their enzymes change, and saliva becomes Ajax. It'll clean anything: a baby's face, a countertop, a Buick—you get enough mothers, you could do a whole car in 30, 40 minutes.

And the best part is, it doesn't even have to be your mother. I go up to total strangers: "Miss, do you have kids? You do? Could you spit on this? I can't get it out."

My wife and I are lucky; we agree on the baby thing. We both want to have kids, and we both don't want to have them *yet*. We feel we should get our relationship, our work, our families, and the universe in order before we jump into anything crazy.

Admittedly, this indulgent, post–baby boom, dual ca-
reer, overthinking, let's-make-everything-perfect-before-
we-bring-anyone-new-into-the-picture plan of attack was
not something they did in the 1200s. I'm pretty sure you
never heard couples in the fiefdoms of Europe saying, "I
just want to get promoted from Serf to Peasant before we
take on the responsibility. . . . If I can just make Execu-
tive Bumpkin before I'm 35, I think I'll be ready. . . .
And *you're* out of town so much now, what with the Cru-
sades and all. . . ."

We both swear that when we *do* have a baby, we're not
going to be obnoxious about it; we're not going to be one
of those couples who whip out the wallet and shove their
baby pictures down your throat.

"Look at this kid—is that beautiful or what?"

They force you into a compliment.

"Is this kid beautiful, or is this kid beautiful?"

I always ask to hear the choices again, because they
sound *so* similar.

The truth of the matter is, sometimes it's *not* a beautiful baby. And I can't lie. I tell them right to their face,
"No, that's a *monkey* you've got there. I wouldn't have
said anything, but you hound me and you hound me, so
now I'm going to tell you: You have yourself a little monkey there. And let me tell you *why:* He's an hour and a half

old in this photo, so you may notice his eyes are not formed yet—*that's* unappealing; his ears are somehow not touching his head, they're kind of hovering around his skull. And, furthermore, his knuckles are scraping the floor. These are signs of having a monkey. Now put the picture away so I can finish my lunch."

Then you feel terrible, so you try to say something positive: "Hey, it's a nice wallet. . . . I'll give you that. . . ." Try to keep the friendship alive.

And it's not just one or two pictures; they take a shot every nine seconds. For new parents, every event is a photo-op.

"Here's him coming into the world, here's him getting toweled down. . . . Here's him eating his first meal, here's the elimination of that very same meal. . . ." They document *everything*.

But you'll notice this slows down with each kid. The second kid gets a little less coverage, the third kid even less. . . . A fifth or sixth kid has virtually *no* photos taken. Maybe one last shot of him running away from home. "You see the bus station? You see the gray jacket in front? That's Tommy lunging for a Greyhound."

When I was a kid, my father was a big picture taker, but he was never *in* the pictures. Sometimes you'd recognize a piece of his thumb, blocking the lens, but that was about it. That's all future generations will have to go on. "You see that beige blur? That's your great-grandfather. Look at your thumb—is that a family resemblance or what?"

And I'll tell you something else about fathers: They never take pictures for the sake of beauty; they need to see relatives. They've got to put at least *one* family member in every shot. It's never, "Oooh, isn't that a spectacular vista." It's, "Oooh, you and your mother go stand *next* to the vista." "Stand with your sister near the sinking sun."

That's why they never get those once-in-a-lifetime shots—they're too busy moving people around.

"Hey, Dad, grab your camera—there's Big Foot!"

"Okay, go stand next to Big Foot."

"But, Dad, he's getting away. . . ."

"Well, hurry up then. I want to get the two of you together, otherwise what's the point? You won't appreciate the height difference . . . that's nice . . . now smile."

See, that's another reason I'm putting off having kids: I don't want to be the grown-up that some fourteen-year-old is rolling their eyes about. And you know it's going to happen.

Because when you're a kid, for a couple of years, no matter how wonderful and loving your parents are, you'd trade them for your friends' parents in a second. Friends' parents always seem cooler than your own parents. Life just looked better over there.

Ironically, your friends always wanted *your* parents.

"Oh, your mom is so great."

"Okay, yeah, but not all the time."

"And your dad's so funny—"

"No, he's not, he's really not. Just when people are around. Seriously, it's a show."

I've always thought they should have an exchange program where family members could *switch* for a while so you could appreciate your own. Just for a day.

Your friend would call you up in a matter of hours: "Could you take your dad back now? He's annoying everybody. We didn't realize he only had that one joke. . . . We thought it was a *series* of funny things."

"What did I try to tell you?"

And the truth is, we know we're going to be *exactly* like our parents.

I'm already starting to *drive* like my father. He wasn't a particularly *bad* driver, it's just that he had different Driving Priorities. For example, being in any one particular *lane* wasn't such a big deal. His attitude was, "Hey, I'm going in the same direction as practically everybody here."

I don't do that yet, but I *do* chase cars for miles just

to tell them their lights are on. I do leave the radio on stations I'm not listening to. And when I make sudden stops, I do shoot my right arm out automatically, even when there's nobody sitting there. I punch the seat—just to be safe.

Did you know, by the way, that this is the leading cause of passenger injury? The Protective Slam of the Driver's Fist? It's true. More damaging than whatever collision they were trying to prevent. BAMM! "Well, Dad, you missed the Buick, but you got my *lungs* pretty good there. . . . As long as we're going by the hospital, why don't we stop and get your *watch* taken out of my heart."

And I'm starting to watch TV like my parents. Whenever they watched movies together, they never commented on the movie itself. Just the actors, and usually only about their age.

"Oh, *he* was younger, huh?"

"Look at that Melvyn Douglas, how young he looks there."

"Boy, *she's* really gotten old, huh? . . . She used to be *my* age."

Or, my favorite: "You know, he's no spring chicken."

"Lena Horne? God bless her—she's no spring chicken."

Spring Chickens are evidently things that people are "not." You never hear about people who *are* Spring Chickens.

You don't watch a movie with Macaulay Culkin and say, "Wow, he is currently a Spring Chicken." But wait till you're watching *Home Alone 25*. See if you don't turn to your kids and say, "You know, he's no spring chicken. . . ."

Ideally, they should give you a couple of "practice kids" before you have any for real. Sort of like bowling a few frames for free before you start keeping score. Let you warm up.

I used to think having a dog was adequate preparation for parenthood, but I'm told they're not exactly the same—pet ownership and child rearing. As I understand it, you can't just leave out a bowl of water and trust that children will entertain themselves by licking their stomachs and chasing a squirrel.

Also, if a child does something they shouldn't—like, oh let's say, steal a car—you can't just whack them on the nose with the Sports Section and say, "What-did-you-do?!" It's not an effective deterrent.

And there's the responsibility. If I'm ever even remotely negligent with the dog, it just confirms my suspicion that I'm not ready for kids.

"I can't believe I just left the dog in the closet for an hour and a half."

"You didn't do it on purpose."

"I know, but what if that was our child? Say our son was chasing a squeaky toy and fell asleep behind our shoes . . ."

"Kids don't do that."

"Yeah, well, still . . . I think we should wait."

Sometimes, I think I'm ready. I'll play with someone else's baby and think, "Hey, this isn't bad. . . . They're cute, they smell like soap, and this one seems to really enjoy me. What the heck—let's do it."

Then, I find out something really fundamental like, "Babies wake up in the middle of the night," and it's all off.

"Oh, yeah, right—okay, let's *not* do it. . . . I forgot about the middle-of-the-night thing. . . ."

Also, I keep thinking that I don't know enough to be anyone's parent. Because kids ask a lot of questions, and I'll be honest with you—I know virtually nothing.

I don't know why planes stay in the air.

I don't know why driving back from somewhere takes less time than driving there.

I don't know why after rain showers it smells like that.

I don't know how you can tell from the outside of a grapefruit if the inside is going to be pink or not.

What if my kid wants to know?

I grew up thinking my parents knew everything. I'm sure they didn't, but at least they were smart enough to fake it. I don't even know how to do that yet.

I have a great fear of just how much I *don't* know.

Have you ever looked in an encyclopedia and seen a picture of Neanderthal Man? (I'm asking this for a reason; go with me for a second.) In every picture, it's the same guy. Evidently, they only dug up one Neanderthal to represent the whole group.

I have this nightmare that thousands of years from now, they're going to dig *me* up to be Mr. Twentieth Century guy. And I won't be able to answer any of their questions.

They'll say, "Well, didn't you live in the twentieth century?"

And I'd tell them, "Yeah, but I wasn't paying attention. I didn't know there was going to be a quiz, so I didn't take notes the whole time I was there. I was sorta taking it pass/fail. . . . I'll try to help you out. What did you want to know?"

"Just a few things: How did they get sweaters from sheep?"

"I don't know. The stores already did it for us. We didn't have to actually yank the wool ourselves."

"How did they get water from the river cleaned up by the time it came out of your faucet?"

"Um . . . some sort of pipe, I'm guessing. I don't know."

"How come electricity never fell out of those little socket holes in the wall?"

"Um, once again—I don't know. There was a switch, that when you put it up, it would just kind of stay, and—I don't know."

"How did those skyscrapers get built?"

"Uh . . . They dig a big hole, and men wearing metal hats would whistle at women for a couple of months. . . . I don't know, I didn't work in that area."

"Is there anything you *do* know?"

"Yeah, I'm pretty sure I'm not ready to have kids yet."

I'll See You

in My

Dreams

———————————Every night, by the time you climb into bed, the day has generally taken such a bite out of both of you that the chances of feeling loving and affectionate can be pretty remote. To combat this, we have a rule:

No discussing Things We Have to Do or Unpleasant Business once we get into bed. Unless it's really important. Or you meant to say it before and didn't get a chance. Or you just feel like saying it for no real reason. (We're nothing if not flexible.)

Originally the plan was, no discussion of unpleasantries *while getting ready for bed,* but that's too hard. There's something about putting a toothbrush in your mouth that makes people want to talk.

Consequently, even the most important exchanges take place between rinsing and spitting.

"I saw that doctor today. . . ." Spit.

"Yeah?" Swish, swish, spit.

"Yeah." Little spit. "He said it's nothing." Big spit.

"Well, *I* say,"—little dribble—"we get a second opinion." Gargle, gargle, cchhwip, pttooey.

(Incidentally, *Cchhwip Pttooey* is not only the sound of someone spitting, but, interestingly enough, the Minister of the Interior of Sri Lanka.)

Every night, you brush and talk and spit and catch up, racing to beat that Conversation Curfew.

See, you don't want to drag the world into bed with you, because there's enough going on there already. Beds are complex, multipurpose arenas, and it's important that the two parties specify which activity they're undertaking.

"Are we talking, or are we reading?"

"Are we sleeping, or are we fooling around?"

You have to clarify.

"Are we not talking because we're mad, or because we both just don't feel like talking?"

"Are we thinking *ambitious* fooling around or *let's just do what we've got to do, and not kill ourselves*?"

The good thing is, when you're together forever, there's less pressure to make any given night magical. You always know you have another shot tomorrow. And the next night.

That's the whole beauty of Forever—nothing but tomorrows.

Of course, if you cash in the Tomorrow Chip too often, you break the bank. One day you roll over, notice each other, and say, "Hey, we used to do something here involving rubbing and touching—any idea what it was? No recollection at all? Hmm . . . I know I enjoyed it, I remember that."

So you negotiate, you clarify, and settle in. You find your position, you fix your pillows, and arrange your mutual blanket.

That blanket, essentially, *is* your relationship: one big cover concealing the fact that two people are inside, squirming around each other trying to get comfortable.

How you handle that blanket is crucial.

Sometimes I wake up and I have *no* blanket. There's nothing there to handle. The woman of my dreams, who is sleeping very cozily, has somehow accumulated the bulk of what's at least half mine.

I tug at it gingerly. She stirs, and seemingly unaware, she tightens her grasp and rolls farther away, taking with her another good foot and a half of blanket. I watch her and calculate my options. I decide it's not worth waking her up or being spiteful, so I try to make do without.

I stare at the ceiling and count the little paint bumps, hoping I can bore myself back to sleep. Within seconds, my brain comes up with five different parts of the house that need painting and fixing, and then I think about how the guy at the hardware store who was so helpful doesn't work there anymore and how the new guy is really unctuous, and I should probably find someplace else. It's 3:25 in the morning and I'm looking for new hardware stores.

Now I'm more irritated and much more awake. I look over and see my bride dreaming blissfully, secure, cradled and warmed by what is now over 90 percent of the blanket. Despite my affection, I resent her deeply.

I sit up. I look at her. I watch her sleep. I think to myself, "How can this be? After all the negotiating and maneuvering and tap dancing we've done, how is it that this person, who, by my own initiative, will be placing her head twelve inches away from *my* head for the rest of my life, is getting such a better end of the bargain? It just doesn't seem right. Will we never get better at this? Must one of us always be less content than the other?"

I pull up the pathetically small segment of blanket left available to me and scoot up next to the woman of my dreams, partly because I hope that her sleep will rub off on me, and partly because I figure she's got to be warmer than *I* am.

And as I hold her close against me, it dawns on me: *Now* I remember. *This* is why we go through all of *that.* Because holding The One Who Fits in your arms simply feels this good, and nothing else really does. And to earn *this,* you must swat away all that stands in its way.

At this point, my wife senses I'm staring at her and opens one eye.

"What," she says.

I say, "What do you mean 'what'?"

"What are you doing?"

"Nothing."

"What are you looking at me for?"

"I wasn't looking. . . . I was just thinking . . . are you really going to be right there every night?"

"Yes."

"Forever?"

"Mm hmm."

"You're saying, that of all the people in the world, the one to whom you will donate your Naked Self, night after night, is *me*?"

"Uh-huh."

If I let it go there, it would have been a nice moment.

"And the reason would be what—because I'm *that* appealing?"

Now she opens both eyes, props herself up on her elbow, and before she can say anything, I say, "I went too far, I see that now. You just go back to sleep, and I'll say nothing."

She slides toward me, and we find homes for our arms and legs. Before long, we're sleeping.

And in the morning, the dance continues.